From the Desk to the Dojang

DAVID IANETTA

David Ianetta From the Desk to the DoJang

Copyright © 2018 by David Ianetta. All rights reserved.

Visit www.davidianetta.com for more information.

November, 2018 REV

No part of this publication may be reproduced, stored in a retrieval system or transmitted in any way by any means, electronic, mechanical, photocopy, recording or otherwise without the prior permission of the author except as provided by USA copyright law.

Book design copyright © 2018 David Ianetta, LLC. All rights reserved.

Cover design by David Ianetta Interior design by David Ianetta November 2018 REV Published in the United states of America

Copyright © 2018 Author David Ianetta

All rights reserved.

ISBN-10:1729670288:
ISBN-13: 978-1729670286

SPECIAL THANKS

I would like to thank first my wife, Rika , who continues to encourage me every step of the way.

I would like to thank my friend Rick Ponger, 3rd Dan , who has been a constant source of encouragement and knowledge.

I would like to thank Master Kim and Master Lee for providing a school and bringing their passion and expertise from South Korea to a small town in North Carolina, USA.

I would like to thank Master Hong whom I had the privilege of studying under before he moved to Texas to start his own school.

I would like to thank Master Won, who was always quick to encourage and share her knowledge with me.

And I would especially like to thank Master Ko whom I am privilege to have instruct me not only in group classes but in private lessons. To me, Master Ko embodies the true spirit of Teakwondo, he is a fountain of knowledge and encouragement to me.

"Taekwondo begins and ends with respect".
-Grandmaster Y.S. Kim

"Venture into the unknown of your potential; you will surely come out the victor."
-Master Sang Kyu Shim

"A black belt is a white belt who never gave up."

-Unknown

WHY AM I HERE?

Master Lee smiled as she handed me a uniform and showed me where to change for my first Taekwondo class. "If you need help tying your belt, I will show you," she said.

I smiled back, awkwardly bowed, and went into the room to change.

Why am I doing this? Why am I here?

I put on the gleaming white uniform and tied the white belt around my waste. My hands tied the belt effortlessly, just as they had done times beyond counting, 32 years ago.

32 years ago, in 1983, I was 18.

Do the math, yeah this year I turned 50.

Fifty...Fifty!

Why am I doing this? Why am I here?

Something has haunted me, for the past 35 years. It nagged away at me as I raised my two sons to adult hood. It's there in the back of my mind whenever I watch a movie with Martial Arts in it. Sometimes I even dream about it. You know those kinds of dreams that teleport you back in time and are full of emotions and vivid images of a time long forgotten.

I quit doing something I loved. I came very close to achieving the goal of getting my Black Belt in Tang Soo Do. However after almost three solid years of study and practice I quit.

I just quit.

Something happened to me that I will share in a later blog. One event caused the passion to die in a moment. One day I looked around the dojang after class, descended the four flights of stairs and exited Byrnes Tang Soo Do in Medford Mass never to return.

Tonight I walked out of the dressing room into the dojang of World Champion Taekwondo in Fuquay NC feeling a little self-conscious in my new uniform. Most of the class are much younger than I.

Many are children.

Why am I doing this? Why am I here?

I sat on the floor, began to stretch out.

At 50, I'm not in too bad of shape. I walk three to five days a week. I do pushups and sit ups regularly. I try to watch what I eat. But the older I get, the more I realize I need something to do that will keep me in better shape the rest of my life.

I tried weights, jogging, even a few classes of yoga. But nothing lasted, I bored too quickly, lacking the passion for those activities to continue.

I do need to take care of my body, is that why I'm here?

The question remained.

Why am I doing this? Why am I here?

I sat up for a moment taking in the dojang. One wall was all mirrored. Another had the ten Student Commitments written there in big bold letter.

I read through the list, and I found my answer at the bottom.

"Always finish what I start."

And now I know.

That's why I'm here. I need to finish what I started as a teenager. I need to push my body and my mind once again. I want to regain the passion I had for martial arts. I want to revive what I allowed to die all those years ago.

This book is my journey. I am committed to getting my Black Belt in Taekwondo. Tang Soo Do was very similar to its better known cousin. Both are Korean Martial Arts.

The school I have found is a traditional one, just like the school I attended all those years ago.

So the journey begins. I'm going to see if I can regain the skill level I once had, and beyond it.

This is a personal journey for me. I'm reconnecting to something I loved and something I was good at. To something that gave me two great friends I still have in my life today. Joe and Bobby, I hope you enjoy reading this!

We all have something like that don't we? An unfinished education, a musical instrument stuck in a case tucked under a bed somewhere. There are unwritten songs and unfinished novel taunting us in those quiet moments. Then there are those dreams placed on hold because we allowed people, events or even just life to get in the way of pursuing them.

This part of my journey is centered on me getting my black belt. I am starting from the beginning. The average time takes 3 years and I plan to blog on this every few weeks to journal my adventure.

Perhaps some of you will see this as my leaving markers along the way. Maybe they will help you, my reader, to rekindle something inside yourself.

Perhaps dust off a dream once again.

I look at the young person I was in these photos. There is nothing I can say to him to tell him not to quit. But perhaps I can do him a favor by putting on this uniform and taking this journey, one day at a time. Maybe I can learn more about who I was then, and who I am today.

"ARE YOU OK, MR. DAVID?"

"Slow down Mr. David"

"Are you OK Mr. David?"

"You can stop for a minute if you like, Mr. David."

Master Hong is a 5th Degree Black Belt. He has a very positive energy about him. He is patient and charismatic. I have learned he is roughly thirty years old.

Ironically that means he was born around the time I quit Tang Soo Do.

Let's not go there!

Master Hong is always aware of what every student is doing in the classroom. I think he may be secretly concerned I will overdo it and die in the middle of class. Perhaps in Korea that is considered bad manners so I will do my best to listen to him, slow down and stay alive!

The first half of the class is a combination of stretching and calisthenics. Then we move on to pairing up with another student or higher rank to learn forms or work on another exercise.

Sometimes we sit and watch or listen. I like that part as I often need to breath or restart my heart.

I have learned Basic Form One. It is comprised of four different blocks and one punch. Each is performed in sequence alternating hands so that you end up with ten moves.

Basic Form One is performed in a stance called a horse riding stance. Basically you bend your legs as if you are riding a horse, then you take away the horse.

Yeah, it sucks.

I was trying to get a current photo of me but my legs were vibrating so fast it created a blurry image even with high shutter speed!

Sigh

So the good news is I have gotten several comments on how advanced my form looks.

The muscle memory is simply there. The blocks and punches snap into place as they once did all those years ago. I realized just how good my training must have been back then to make this possible 30 years later. Kathy Gallager and Richard Byrnes were excellent instructors the credit truly goes to them.

On class this past week we worked on Basic Form One together as a group. I was asked with a higher belt to demonstrate form one for the whole class. Nervousness kicked in and I made one mistake, but it still felt good when everyone applauded us.

So my form is not bad (yet there is always room for improvement), but the body strength is not what it needs to be. During the class my legs constantly want to give out. As I write this, they are aching.

After the first few classes I limped around work, my legs ached that much. No sharp pain, it is just obvious I am using muscles I have not used in a long time.

Seeing how Taekwondo is about 70% kicking, I need the strength and flexibility to do this correctly.

A fellow student suggested I sit with my back against a wall in an "imaginary chair" to build leg strength. I try to steal away a few times at work each day to do this. It has proven helpful but I do feel I have a long way to go.

I love being back in the classroom. My fellow students are helpful and encouraging. After class all of the stress of the day seems to vanish and I am energized.

So far so good. I just missed a promotion cycle, the next one is in two months. Although my goal is to get that Black Belt, I am really just focusing on doing everything I learn, the best that I can.

I CAN DO IT, YOU CAN DO IT, WE CAN DO IT!

Last night we went over the Round House Kick.

I am shocked how much I have lost in 30 years. No matter how hard I tried, I could not execute this kick correctly. My legs flopped around with little to no focus. This is the first time I had to fight some discouragement.

I think this hits me the hardest because at one time I won first place in a tournament with this kick. I broke two boards that were held about a foot higher than my head. The regret of quitting all those years ago was rising up inside me.

My first concern was that my hips simply lack the flexibility I will need and that this might be irreversible.

I was tempted to start Googling around to see if it is possible to ever regain that kind of control again. I decided against that. I want to shoot for being the best I can be, and that means I don't want to put any limits on what I can achieve.

At the end of each class a student is chosen to lead the class in a series of shouts. First the student shouts, next the whole class repeats it.

"I can do it!"
"You can do it!"
"We can do it!"
"We are the best! We are the Champions!"

I left the class with those shouts ringing in my ears.

So after trying it at home, slowly step by step I did realize I was doing something wrong in class.

When lifting my kicking leg, I had been leaving my supporting foot forward. By lifting and turning my foot at the same time, the move became much easier. I am still only kicking waist high but I can do this!

Still leg strength has some influence on my technique looking sloppy. After each kick is executed my leg gets more and more fatigued. But I am confident this will come in time.

So, this week I had a little discouragement, but I'm sticking with it and moving forward!.

"MR DAVID, PUT SOME ICE ON THAT WHEN YOU GET HOME"

Tonight's class started out great.

I have some upper body strength and made it through the pushups while my partner held my legs in the air rather well. And when we lined up and did punches, my uniform sleeve gave that nice "snapping" sound it is supposed to when you throw a good punch.

I was rather pleased with myself. Maybe too pleased...

Then we worked on the Side Kick.

To do a proper Side Kick, you have to start with your supporting foot, toes facing forward. Then, as you bring your kicking leg up, those toes end up facing backwards as you kick your leg out.

Master Hong effortlessly demonstrated this for the whole class. He is very good at explaining this and makes it simple to understand.

My mind agreed as I said, "Yes Sir!" with the rest of the class when he asked, "Can you do this?"

Then it was time to execute.

Well.

Sometimes my past training works against me. The mind says, "this is how things should go, one smooth move, you've done this thousands of times now GO…"

But the body quickly adds, "yes, but that was a thousand years ago!"

My foot did not turn all the way as it should. The rest of my body tried fall in line with what my mind told it to do. But my foot had other plans. It moved only half way and then decided to stop.

This resulted in a slight twist in my Achilles tendon.

The first thought that ran through my head was, UH OH, I really did something to my body this time! What was I thinking!!!

Master Hong noticed I was not kicking with everyone else, but trying to stretch out the tendon that wanted to ball up and pull my toes somewhere back into my foot. When I explained the injury he looked concerned.

"Sit down please, sir"

I sat.

We moved onto doing the Side Kick from a sitting position and my tendon throbbed less and less. I sighed with relief. The injury doesn't appear to be too bad, and my next class is Saturday. I have time to heal before then.

Now I sit at home, with ice on my tendon as Master Hong suggested, flipping through TKD Times Magazine.

The biggest challenge for me will be my leg strength. Building up the strength and flexibility needed.

I'm not discouraged by this at all. I realize that, yes I can do this. I just have to remember, getting the Black Belt is a marathon, not a sprint. I need to let go of the thought of where I should be and focus on where I am.

Today that is the lesson I am learning. Focusing on the now. Not on the technique that was lost or where I should be. But focus on where I am and what I am trying to accomplish today.

One month into my goal, I love it more each day!

"HUMILITY, SIR!"

At the end of every class we call out the "Five aims of Taekwondo."

"Aim number three?"

"Humility, sir!"

My wife and I were at Home Depot the other day when a man approached us with his nine year old son. He had a great big smile on his face. Obviously he knew me from somewhere but I had no idea who he was.

"Hey, don't you take Taekwondo with my son?"

"Um… yes I do," I answered.

"I thought I saw you when I was watching my son's class!" He looked at me, then at my wife, "So, how do you like it?"

"Oh, I love it," I told him.

"My son does too."

There was an awkward silence where I thought for a moment he was going to ask my wife if they could arrange a play date for me the boy!

His son, who I am reasonably sure, is a higher belt than I am. I honestly couldn't say. There are so many kids in the class at times I can't tell one from the other.

There may have been a time when this would have bothered me, but not anymore. I think somewhere along my journey to adulthood I left being self-consciousness far behind me.

I often see the parents watching the class. How many would love to join in?

I wonder how many people allow fear of what others might think prevent them from running after their goals? Or perhaps it is simply a lack of humility that stops them learning something new?

I often told my sons, who are now grown men, " Keep a small list of people whose opinions truly matter to you, and everyone else is not on that list."

Fear of what other think can cripple dreams.

So yes, I find it amusing that I am in a class with mostly kids. However, I enjoy their youthful enthusiasm. I also enjoy seeing young people do something besides play video games. It restores my faith in the next generation.

The few adults I have come to get to know have been a great source of encouragement to me as well. More than once I have gotten great advice on how to work out my body as it adjusts to the new strain I have placed on it.

Humility is actually "strength under control." So if being in a class with a bunch of kids running circles around me (literally when we jog around the class) helps me practice Humility, so much the better!

I'm having a great time, doing something I love. And really, that's all that matters.

6 SIX WEEKS INTO MY BLACK BELT JOURNEY, ALREADY REAPING THE BENEFITS.

What has TKD given me so far, in six short weeks?

A tangible purpose for health.

Before stepping into class almost six weeks ago my exercising habits were sketchy and random at best. Occasionally I did sit-ups, pushups, maybe I stretched a little. I walk at lunch at work if the weather allows. But nothing really too challenging, and quite frankly these activities bored me.

My eating habits were mostly good. But again I had no tangible goal to obtain. Just a vague knowledge that somehow I am doing my body some future good and I want that. Storing up health points like pennies in a piggy bank. They feel like they will never really add up to something, but it's still a good idea.

So what did TKD change?

Let's step back in time again…

When I was a teenager practicing martial arts, I had no idea the kind of shape I was in. I was too busy trying to perfect the next form, the next kick or spar smarter. (I grew up in Boston, so you have to pronounce that last one SPA SMATA as my teenage self would have said).

Teenagers, sigh… they believe they will live fA EvA.

This brings me to an unexpected benefit given to me by TKD. I now have a tangible reason to stay in shape.

Why am I going into the stairwell at work to stretch and exercise my Achilles tendon three times a day? TKD. Why did I not snack the other night? Just got back from TKD. Why am I doing more sit-ups? TKD.

You get the idea.

For me, staying in shape, just for the sake of staying in shape is not enough of a motivation factor.

But during TKD class I want to perform better. I want my legs to not want to give out when I try to kick and I want my feet to feel stable and strong.

A healthy stronger body is important to me, in class. Therefore I change my habits outside of class.

Yes, I do have the goal of getting my Black Belt, however I plan to keep this up fA EvA.e.

GETTING STRONG NOW...

Tonight I earned my yellow belt tip. This marks the first change in my belt since the journey began.

A yellow belt tip is for learning the form. Blue is for kicking, footwork, sparring and self-defense, and white is for attendance, work habits, conduct and terminology.

When you have one of each color tip, you are given an application to test for the next belt.

Although I am not in a hurry to get my Black Belt (and it's a good thing!) it does feel good to see this splash of color on the white belt. Another step has been taken on this journey.

OK, queue the Rocky theme music here...

See David running around the classroom, getting high fives from Master Hong and Master Beck as he passes them... see that little kid blaze past David...and the next kid... and the next kid... or was it the same kid each time?

Ok... kill the Rocky sound track music!

It has been roughly eight weeks since I started TKD. My body is starting to adjust physically. By that I mean I am no longer limping when I walk! (well, on most days) and I feel less aches and pain after class.

I am still asked often if I am OK, by Master Hong, Master Lee and occasionally even Master Kim.

However when doing sit-ups tonight, Master Hong pushed my shoulders back to make them harder for me. Perhaps he is not as worried about my dying in class as he once appeared to be!

I have discovered a few interesting things about my body so far.

The first thing has been pointed out to me by a fellow student. Because I wear motorcycle boots or dress boots almost all the time, the higher heel has caused my Achilles tendon to shrink over the years. Therefore, walking barefoot on a mat has been stretching the tendon every class as my heel sinks down in. That has been a great source or discomfort for me to say the least!

Fortunately this is not a permanent condition. I was able to find some exercises that I do two to three times a day to stretch and strengthen the tendon.

Basically, I stand on a stair on the balls of my feet. Then I allow my heels to drop below the stair, stretching the tendon. After that I rise as high as I can. I do three sets of about 12 to 15 reps of this.

After about a week, I have seen a marked improvement and the pain is all but gone. Leg strength is still a concern, but I'm working on it daily. I'm beginning to rethink my shoes!

The other lesson I learned was from Master Hong tonight. He was watching my form and noticed that I stayed tense and tight the whole time. This causes me to fatigue much faster. Often after a few times through I am huffing and puffing, catching my breath.

Master Hong showed me how I should keep my body completely relaxed until I am ready to execute my move.

I wondered about that. How often is my body tense when it does not need to be? Does this happen throughout the day too? I'll have to watch and see.

I'm tired tonight, a little sore, but feeling accomplished. I enjoy going to class. Everyone is so helpful and encouraging. After a long day at work, it is a great way to get rid of the stress of the day.

Eight weeks, still going strong!.

GETTING REACQUAINTED WITH OPTIMISM

Tonight I earned my blue tip by demonstrating I now know the kicking forms needed to test for my high white belt(a white belt with a yellow stripe)

One more visible step on the journey!

My wife Rika was very proud of me when I got home tonight since now my belt pays homage to her home country of Sweden. Not exactly what I was going for, but hey I'll take it!

Physically I am still facing little challenges here and there. With all the kicking tonight I am once again making acquaintance with a bag of ice.

(sing to the tune of "Sound of Silence")

Hello ice bag, my old friend
I've come to talk to you again
I have this new pain and it's throbbing
A night of sleep I'm sure It'll be robbing

OK, enough of that!

I don't know how Master Hong does it, but he seems to be very aware of when I am over doing it. I was doing my kicking form 1-

5, over and over and he walked up, watched me do my kicks and then said, "Ok, sit down and stretch sir."

As I began to stretch I felt a pain working up in my upper thigh. By the time I got home, my leg was throbbing. I had been so focused on getting the series of blocks, kicks and punches right that I wasn't paying attention to my body.

Truly my mind wants to push my body harder than it is ready to handle!

As I write this, the ice bag is working its magic.

Over all I do feel I am getting stronger and more flexible. I am happy to report my Achilles tendon is much better and when I bend over to touch my toes, the tips of my fingers almost reach without bending my knees.

Almost...

I like to get to class about ten minutes early to stretch. While I am sitting on the mat, the class before mine is finishing up. Often I learn terminology or correct technique by just watching.

This class is made up of little kids. I think the oldest might be nine or ten.

I love watching them. It is amazing how hard they try. Their little faces all serious and focused one minute burst into a wide smile when Master Hong praises them for doing well. It makes me feel good just to see children doing something so positive. I truly hope they stick with it.

This is something I did not expect taking Taekwondo. The effect is has on me to be surrounded by so much positive energy. As I have gotten older, I realize just how cynical I have become when I see all the bad news in the world around me.

Sometimes as the years pass and we have seen and been through too much life can beat us down. Like my muscles we begin to stiffen and loose our ability to reach beyond our own perspective. Soon our range of motion is limited. Optimism is harder to obtain. Stretching to dream is too painful.

We stiffen. What is true of the body, is true of the mind.

But being in a class with everyone, young and old, sharing a common goal is refreshing. As I stretch and strengthen my body, my world view is finding a place once again for hope.

Taekwondo is about so much more than learning how to fight. It has a ripple affect, like a pebble tossed into a pond, that runs through my whole life.

ONCE UPON A TIME IN MEDFA MASS

I earned my white belt tip and received my invitation for my first belt test!

My body is getting strong, technique appears to be improving. Of my many challenges, my biggest ones are relaxing between blocks and kicks, and learning my Korean terminology!

One of my favorite tv shows when I was a kid was the original Kung Fu.

I used to love the way Cain would see something that would trigger a memory for him of something he learned back in the Shaolin Temple. There would be this long high pitched note as they would flash back and forth until we arrived in the memory.

Since something like that happened to me the other night while I was watching the class before mine finish up, I thought it only fitting to have flash back moments to my days of learning Tang Soo Do in this blog!

I was sitting and stretching. The scent of my freshly washed cotton uniform added to my watching Master Hong teach the children a front kick brought me right back to my first days of Tang Soo Do.

I could see myself, young again wearing that brand new uniform. Sitting, stretching, watching, and learning.

I was a shy teenager who had been getting lost deeper and deeper within himself. The move from a small town to the city had taken its toll on me. I was lost inside myself, shrinking away as each day passed by.

My brother Steven was home on leave from the Army, getting ready to head out to Korea for a year. He came up stairs to my bedroom and noticed how clean it was.

Scary clean and neat; too clean for a teenager and perhaps too clean for an adult as well. That was the first sign something was wrong. Then Steven found out I spent all of my time in that room, lost in books for my imagination. I didn't have any friends and only went to school because I was forced to go.

After talking with my mother, Steven decided to take action. He called my father who agreed to pay for Martial Arts lessons for me.

I remember the day he told me what he had arranged for me.

At the time I was a huge Billy Jack and Bruce Lee fan. And of course, I loved Kung Fu. Although nothing else worked to get me out of the house, the idea of taking Martial Arts was tempting enough for me to face my first fears of leaving the house and walking down that street.

Byrnes Tang So Do was on the 4th Floor.

I remember Steven taking me for a walk. I was full of anxiety just going outside. We walked together, the mile or so to Byrnes Tang Soo Do in Medford Square (locals pronounced that one, Medfa). As we got closer and closer I could see the mural painted on the bottom of the building.

By the magic of Google Maps, I was able to get this current photo. Byrnes Tang Soo Do is no longer on the fourth floor of that old building, but the mural remains to this day.

Steven took me to meet Richard Brynes who shook my hand and welcomed me. I was so shy I could not even look at him. We signed up and I was told they would have a uniform waiting for me that next week for my first class.

I could hardly wait.

The first time I put on the uniform I felt such a surge of excitement in me. I don't remember who showed me my first blocks and stances, but I remember the feeling of watching everyone perform moves that would eventually become so familiar to me I could do them in my sleep.

As the classes built onto each other, my self-confidence grew and I broke out of my shell. I met my friends Bobby and Joe who are, to this day, still in my life although we live in different states.

Martial Arts in many ways shaped who I was back then, and who I am today.

It's an interesting thing to returning to a passion after this many years. I am still only learning what this means to me.

My body is still sore after class, but heart is glad.

I am happy to be back.

YOU'RE THE BEST!

So, you know how in many of the movies like "Rocky" or "Karate Kid" they play a montage? A series of scenes that represent a certain amount of time to move the story along for the viewer.

Well, here is a montage of journey so far.

You can choose any music you like while reading, just don't think about "You're the best!" from Karate kid because that's just too corny.

Crap, it's already in your head isn't it?

Oh well….here we go!

"You're the best!"

See David going into the stairwell at work doing dips, he switches to one leg at time….see him limping back to his desk…(you're the best) see David trying to stretch while Master Hong catches his efforts and the pain in his face, "Very good Mr David!" he says with laughter in his voice…(around! No one's ever gonna get you down!) see David at home that night with a bag of ice on his ankle…(You're the best!)… hear Master Hong over and over, "Are you OK Mr David?"

See David standing in a horse riding stance with his legs vibrating so much you could play one of those tiny football games on his thighs….don't know what I'm talking about? Ask your Dad…(you're the best!) See David getting stronger, no longer limping every day. See David kicking more and more and not ending up in pain the day after class…See David get his final belt tip and be invited to test for his first belt.

See David come home from class and not have to ice any part of his body.

Cut the music.

Seriously…stop singing that song. Now it's in my head, stuck there, over and over.

Sigh

Ok, on to tonight.

One of the aspects I love the most about Taekwondo is the attention to detail.

Tonight we had a much smaller class, most of the students were advanced. So tonight's class paid careful attention to details of various stances and kicks.

Every move is precise, every part of the body has a place where it needs to be. The steps to execute each have a reason, and when they all come together the body is in perfect harmony and it works.

When you see a master perform the moves it is beautiful to watch, like a dance. The more you learn, the more you know what to watch for and can appreciate the art.

Tonight Master Hong was working with me on my round house kick. He pointed out that I had neglected one small detail with my kicking foot in regard to knee placement as my foot comes up. Once that got corrected, the whole kick became much smoother! So that was awesome to discover!

Edgar Degas said, "Art is not what you see, but what your make others see." That can be true of our lives as well. It is not about what we can do well, but by what we can contribute to others to enrich their lives.

One of the most rewarding experiences for me so far in this Black Belt Journey came when a co-worker returned to martial arts after reading my blog. To see his face light up as he told me about his classes, that was an amazing feeling. I don't know how many out there are reading this, but that one person made blogging this journey worthwhile for me.

So what is it you love to do? What do you need to return to?

After all…YOU'RE THE BEST!

DAVID IANETTA

FEMALE MARTIAL ARTISTS

Tonight the class was divided up into kids and adults. Master Hong took the children and the adults got Master Lee.

Master Lee was the first female member of the Tae Kwon Do team at the Korea National Sport University, a 5th Degree KUKKIWON Black Belt and a Kickboxing/Aerobics Instructor.

With her leading the class, we did not stop moving all night, and my legs are still shaking as I write this! Don't let the disarming smile fool you, this is one tough lady!

Great workout! I was happy to actually make it through the entire class without passing out. My overall fitness must be improving. I'm very fortunate this class was not my first, I might be blogging about basket weaving or something.

Well, maybe not basket weaving, per se... but something much less physical!

My first instructor was also a woman, Kathy Gallegar.

At the time Kathy was in her mid-twenties and a second degree black belt. She could not have been taller than five feet, but was able to break something like four boards with a jump back kick.

This was when she returned to Tang Soo Do after having a hip replaced.

She was amazing, a force to be reckoned with.

Like Master Lee, Kathy, could be smiling happy one minute, but very serious about teaching the next. I remember holding my leg out, high in mid-air waiting to hear the command to pull it back down again while it just burned and burned (and that command took a looooong time coming!).

And it is because of the foundation she gave me that I am able to get back into Martial Arts today. The basics are still there.

There really is no difference in Taekwondo between men and women, both are capable of doing amazing things. In class we work together, and push toward the same goals.

This kind of atmosphere is great for fostering mutual respect and support between men and women. I wish there were more sports like it.

And to be honest, I think I will have a private sigh of relief if Master Lee doesn't run the next class!

Getting stronger, looking forward to my first test!

TESTING DAY FOR MY FIRST BELT

Even though I am fairly confident I will walk away this evening with my new belt (White with a yellow stripe) I am surprisingly nervous. I have worked pretty hard over the past few months to get to this point and be allowed to test. I remember all my moves and I have learned my Korean terminology.

But the dojang has been transformed into a testing room with a very official-looking table.

Seeing that table and recalling past tests, I am suddenly nervous.

Master Kim is sitting at a table and there are a lot of visitors watching friends and family members. My wife, Rika, is among them. I have to tell myself to focus on what I am doing and not pay attention to the audience.

There are about twenty five of us testing, all ranks. Everyone, from white belts like mine to higher belts, is testing.

They separate us by belts so I have a young boy who looks to be about seven or eight, sitting next to me. It's hard not to be a little self-conscious knowing how glaringly obvious it is that I am by far the oldest person testing!

After watching some of the higher ranks perform forms and kicks, my name is called.

"Mister David," Master Kim says into a microphone.

"Yes, sir!"

Now I am standing in the middle of the room, all eyes are on me.

First I perform Basic Form One while Master Kim counts out for me. I remember all my moves and I'm feeling pretty good about that.

Next I am asked to demonstrate the Taekwondo combination (block, punch, kick) and my one-step sparring comprises of kicks and punches (1-5).

Master Kim has not observed my technique before. He normally oversees the higher rank classes and I am very pleased to hear him say, "wow!" a few times.

The affirmation feels good.

You're the best! (Karate Kid reference.... don't get that song in my head again...)

Of course, during all the activity I forget to relax my body between moves, and I am tense the whole time. When I finish I am standing there breathing heavily. Master Kim asks, into that same microphone, "Do we need to call 911?"

Laughs from all... and I join in the laughter, "I get that question a lot!"

Next comes some sparring. I am matched up with a teenager who is a much higher rank. I'm very happy they don't match me up with that seven-year old for this!

I recall one of the only other times I sparred and how tired I got after that first time. This is light sparring, no equipment. But this time I remember to relax and I do rather well against my much younger opponent. I realize that all the work I have done up to this point has actually paid off!

Then comes something I am not expecting. Board breaking. Up until this point I have not attended a class where we have broken a board. I have not kicked or punched a board in over 30 years.

The black belt assisting me is a gentleman about my age and a very nice man. He coaches me through the first board. Basically a hammer fist down on the board and I break it easily.

But then I hear Master Kim tell him to hold two boards that I am asked to break with a push kick.

In Tang Soo Do there was no push kick. The push kick is quite different from the front kick I knew, mainly regarding foot position. Here I should kick with the flat of the foot, whereas I learned to pull my toes back and kick with the ball of my foot.

Two boards are facing me, held a little higher than my waist. I'm not really comfortable with this flat foot thing so I decide to go with what I know, but will my toes still pull back and expose the ball of my foot to hit the target?

I know when I commit to this kick there is no turning back. Something is going to break tonight and I hope it won't be my toes!

I give a strong yell and let my foot fly.

Snap!

Both boards break and I have to say, I feel great!

The test is almost over and now we are tested on terminology. I answer the questions correctly and I sit back down. Having gone first, I listen as each student is asked terminology questions, or about their life goals.

Then something happens that I don't expect. Master Kim asks me to stand, a second time.

I think I made him curious. Although my body is not what it once was, it is obvious from my technique that I have studied martial arts before. Master Kim asks me about this; I tell him I studied Tang Soo do some thirty years ago. He obviously is familiar with this style too.

"And what is your short-term goal, Mister David?"

I think for a minute. I have so many goals I don't even know which one to choose.

So I smile and say, "to make it through the next class!"

Although Master Kim smiles at my comment, he isn't letting me off that easily. "And what is your long-term goal, Mister David?"

"To finish what I started 30 years ago." I tell him.

After that each of us are called up, and handed the new belt by Master Kim. Then together we take off the old belt, and put on the new.

I'm looking now at my new belt, white, with a yellow strip running along lengthwise.

There are many belts between this one and that black belt. But there is an old saying, "A journey of a thousand miles begins with a single step.

I can't help but feel proud that I have made it this far

I AM LEARNING TO WALK ALL OVER AGAIN.

Master Hong taught me basic form number two. As the name implies, this form is basic. A series of ten moves compiled of blocks and punches. Now unlike basic form one (which stays in a horse riding stance the entire duration of the form, making me vibrate so much I think I may jack hammer my way through the floor) basic form two takes a step with each block or punch.

The problem for me is that the first five steps are very similar to the basic forms of Tang Soo Do but with one important exception, a different stance is used.

Taekwondo has a walking stance, Tang Soo do used a leaning stance. And here's the funny part. The walking stance is... well... like you are walking. The leanings stance is very different and is actually harder.

However, since 30 years ago, I had the leaning stance drilled into me over and over and over again that is what my body wants to do. A walking stance feels wrong, it feels like a sloppy leaning stance. I feel clumsy and awkward just walking.

But I have accepted that I am learning Taekwondo, and this is the way it is done. So I try over and over to get it right. I have to really concentrate just to... walk.

"No sir," corrects Master Hong, "this is walking stance... like you are walking... just like that..."

I picture myself taking my first steps toward Master Hong like a toddler with a "binky" stuck in my mouth while Master Hong is encouraging me, "Good! Good Mister David!".

Sigh

I am learning to walk all over again.

I wonder how many things are ingrained in us like this?

I have not had a need for that leaning stance in over 30 years. It's not like someone says at a job interview, "Ok, now show me your leaning stance!" It doesn't even come up in normal every day conversation, "Hey David, how's that new leaning stance working out for ya?"

Yet there the habit sat, dormant in me as muscle memory. Turn left, low block, snap into a perfect leaning stance. Problem is what was right then, is wrong now.

Again Master Hong tell me, "No, Sir... a walking stance..."

He is very patient.

How many things in our life are just like that? Habits so ingrained in us that we are not even aware they are there? Change does not come easy, it takes repetition of what is right to correct what was wrong.

I take a breath, and start basic form two again.

I focus on walking...

DID MASTER KIM REALLY SAY, "100 BACK-UPS"?

I made a recent change to my TKD schedule. I'm now going on Tuesday and Thursday nights.

One of the benefits of these classes is the size. They are smaller and set up strictly for teens and adults.

This is both a blessing and a challenge!

The smaller classes mean more attention given to the individual students and more overall room to work out.

However, the absence of younger ones means there are only a few of my rank, and the physical aspects of the class are far more challenging.

I love this; when my brother Michael sat me down and taught me guitar he told me, "If you only play with those you are better than, it will stroke your ego, but if you seek out people who are better than you, those you can learn from, you will always improve."

That was a life lesson, and it applies here as well. I really don't care that almost everyone is a higher belt than myself. The only person I am trying to be better than is the person I was when I walked into the class that night.

Now, Master Hong has been in Korea for the past few weeks, and Master Kim has been teaching the classes.

Master Kim who began studying Taekwondo at age five and graduated from Korea National Sport University #1 in his class. He is a 7th Degree KUKKIWON Black Belt and was a member of Korean Olympic Committee for 10 years.

Although he often motions me to slow down and take it easy, he also pushes me along with the rest of the class to perform harder and better. The physical aspects are far more demanding. At the end of class, when I am soaked through with sweat, we spend the last few minutes going over the exactness of specific techniques.

This is exactly why I practice TKD.

Sure, the health benefits are obvious, cardio, flexibility, and core strength. I know my body has gotten stronger and better in all these areas. That's a plus at my age!

But then there is the discipline of getting the stances, blocks, kicks and other moves just right. Master Kim will point out a subtle correction of hand position, or offer an encouraging word when you get it right.

When we are first born we learn to move. We learn to control our bodies to get around. There is something fundamental in the martial arts when it comes to movement that resonates deep inside me. It makes my hurried and stressed mind relax and focus. The concerns of the day just melt away.

In all of this, I have discovered how much I like to challenge myself physically. And, of course I love to keep learning.

Recently my wife and I went to the National Art Gallery where I bought what has become one of my favorite T-shirts. It has a quote from Michelangelo who was in his later years when he said, "I am still learning."

And I am. I'm learning to push my body beyond the limits I created for it. I'm learning to spend more time doing the things I am passionate about. I'm learning how much just being around the positive atmosphere of my classroom means to me after a long day.

And I'm learning something I always instinctively believed. It's never to late to follow a dream or a passion.

DAVID IANETTA

SAYING GOODBYE TO REGRET

Greig Hochreiter, one of the owners of Devolve Moto, recently said to me, "Regret is poison to the soul."

Sometimes when I think about how I left martial arts, I wish I could go back in time and tell that young man the mistake he is about to make, walking away.

I can still see myself standing at that heavy bag throwing kick after kick, my hard-earned red belt around my waist. I remember knowing, as I folded my uniform and descended the four flights of stairs, that I would never go back.

My body was fit and my technique was very good, but my heart was not in it anymore. Too much of me was working for the approval of someone else. And when I thought that approval was not there, that pain overshadowed any joy I felt over how far I had come.

I could no longer see how much martial arts meant to me. Every kick got harder to throw and I gave up. I walked away.

Life can be like that sometimes. The times when we give up on something and walk away.

Last night I earned my yellow belt! This belt is significant to me because there is no longer any white on it (my previous belt was white with a yellow stripe running through it). The solid color around my waist feels so good because I'm moving forward. No more white on the belt!

I've decided today to leave something else behind, something more than the white in my belt; I'm leaving regret behind. Thoughts like, "where would my technique be today, thirty years later, when I used to be that good?" These are the pointless thoughts of regret and I'm choosing to no longer think them.

We feel regret when we look back on choices we made that cannot be undone. That is where the poison comes from. When we look at a choice and know there is nothing we can do to get that moment back. When we dwell on that one fact, and only that fact, those are the thoughts that can take the joy out of life and prevent us from moving forward.

Life is full of choices, and the only ones we can really do anything about are the ones in front of us today. They will affect our future from here on out. Bad choices in the past should be learned from and never repeated, but not lived in.

Four months ago I made a choice to return to martial arts. Last night I wrapped a yellow belt around my waist. I have earned my second belt in Taekwondo, moving one step closer to my black belt goal.

Often that black belt seems so far out of reach. As a young man, it was so much closer; that black belt was right within my grasp.

Today it is a few years away at best.

I am not the young man who walked away. I am the older (and perhaps somewhat wiser) man today who made the choice to return.

I recently hung a heavy bag in my "man cave/dojo". With each kick I can feel my body and my heart getting stronger.

I've left regret behind me, I'm living, today, fully alive.

DAVID IANETTA

SIX MONTHS IN, TIME FOR SOME REAL SPARRING!

This past week, I arrived at a new milestone in my black belt journey.

After six months, and two belt promotions I have finally been allowed to put on pads and spar with contact!

The whole "pads" thing is new to me. With Tang Soo Do, we never wore pads. Not even in a tournament. The rule of thumb was, "light" contact to the body, no contact to the head. Sure, there were times when we got a little hurt, but nothing too serious. There was a great emphasis on control, and hurting someone else when sparring was looked at as you didn't know what you were doing.

Fast-forward thirty years. In Taekwondo we pad up, just like you see in the Olympics. That means instep pads that go all the way up your shin, hand pads that cover your arms up to your elbows. Then there is chest gear, and finally headgear.

Headgear, really? Do I have to wear that silly thing? I put it on and my wife snickered at me. I felt like the Mike Myers hyper kid "LOOK, My mother says I have to wear a helmet!" There is simply no way to pull off cool wearing this thing.

Did Billy Jack wear headgear? No! Did Cain wear one in Kung fu? No!

But then again, Cain shaved his head bald… I regress.

Oh well, I figured, everyone else wears one, perhaps I won't look so silly… maybe.

My wife still snickered and I lost two "sexy points", I'm sure of it.

Sigh

I ordered my set from the school, and patiently waited until it came. This past week it finally arrived! I looked at all the pads, including… a cup.

Dunt dunt dunt da!!!!

OK, now a cup is not the most comfortable thing in the world to wear, it just is… not!

And they have changed some in the years since I had to wear one. The thing looked like it would go great under some spandex if I were in a heavy metal band… (Maybe I can get my two sexy points back… no… and no!)

So when Thursday night came and it was time to get ready for class, I tossed the cup aside.

Class was brutal, as always. There are usually anywhere from twelve to twenty students, most of them deputy black belts and black belts. This is great for me; I get a good workout trying to keep up!

So then it came time to spar! I suited up, excited that the moment had finally arrived.

I kid you not, the first thing out of one of the black belts' mouth (he's must be about seventeen) was, "Oh, wow, I remember when I first started sparring, I got kicked in the groin like a half a dozen times!"

Then master Hong said, "Yes, I did too when I was six, it hurt!"

This led to a conversation with students sharing similar times they had experienced that made me feel like a certain part of my anatomy now had a bulls-eye painted on it.

I smiled despairingly as Master Hong tightened and tied the back of my chest pads.

Inside my head, all I could see was that cup, sitting uselessly on my dresser at home!

What was I thinking? I haven't sparred for real in over 30 years, and I just left myself unprotected in the worst possible place?

Really?

I was matched up with a 2nd degree black belt known as Mr. Mario. He is everything a black belt should be; strong, confident, good-natured and very good!

Fortunately he took it very easy on me, knowing it was my first time. I have to say, I loved it! Fighting with gear on, making some contact, is a lot of fun! It's much better than doing it without.

I still tense up some, in my upper body, but I'm working on that. And I need to remember to keep moving.

Also, I'm happy to report, I made it through the sparring sessions without any… mishap! You can bet though, I'll wear that cup from now on!

At the end of class, Master Hong talked about how everything we do makes us better when we spar, and how important conditioning is to this. That is something I've noticed, the stronger my legs get, the better my kicks are.

Today is Saturday and I went into the "man-cave/dojo" and worked out with tension kicks and the heavy bag. I did lots of stretching as well as leg conditioning.

Six months in and feeling great! I can't believe I've been at this for half a year!

NO MIND

It's time to take things to another level.

Yes, I've been working hard these past seven months, but now it's time to take things up a notch. I can feel it. There is a resolve in my mind and body. Not some "New Year's resolution" deal, more of an epiphany. My body is ready to move to the next level.

First physically…

A few classes ago we did some concentration work with sidekicks; first from a sitting position and then from a standing position.

Before we began, Master Hong told us we would sleep well that night. He wasn't kidding. Oh sure, he laughed when he said it… but he wasn't joking.

First slow kicks from a sitting position, I don't remember how many we did, maybe thirty with each leg.

Then we stood, holding our legs up and extended the sidekick out, with each leg, for four sets of ten.

With each set, I never set my foot down. After forty sidekicks, with each leg, I was feeling it.

And this was after doing line forms with front kicks, sidekicks and round kicks.

Later that night, legs were still sore as I sat after my shower drinking water.

It was a good soreness, not the kind that comes from pain, but the kind that comes from knowing I worked the muscles to complete failure. The kind of work that means they will grow stronger, and they need to.

And now, I know I need to feel like this more. I need this soreness in order to grow stronger.

Two things I simply need to do more of, stretching and kicking exercises.

First stretching. I don't think I challenge my body enough. I need to push harder in my stretches; especially in my hips. Those are the "hidden" muscles that are preventing me from getting a better form on all my kicks.

Then, simply working harder with my legs. I learned a few exercises that I can do in order to work my legs harder. As long as I lack the flexibility and strength, I will not get the technique I need to advance.

But also, mentally something has changed inside me.

This past week I had an epiphany moment while working on my form for last night's belt test.

There were a lot of students all around me practicing different forms (or poomsae) and at first I found that rather distracting. But then something clicked inside me. I thought only of the next move in the poomsae. My body relaxed and my mind felt at peace. There was no longer any distractions, just the next move, the next kick, the next block. I didn't think ahead if I would remember the whole poomsae, I just focused on the task at hand. I relaxed and put power into the next move, then relaxed, then power. All through the poomsae I did this.

There is a quote from the movie "The Last Samurai" that I finally understood, when Algren is trying to learn the sword. Nobutada runs over to him and says,

Nobutada: "Please forgive; too many mind."
Algren: "Too many mind?"
Nobutada: "Hai, mind the sword, mind the people watch, mind enemy - -too many mind... no mind."

And that is how it felt. Like I realized something about concentrating on one single task, one movement. Living in and for that moment and only that moment. No worry or fear about the next thing to do. Nothing else existed around me, just the task in front of me. I knew I needed to do only that, and do it well.

That is the beauty of Taekwondo to me.

That is what I took with me to my belt test tonight. It's hard for me sometimes as a 50-year old man to test with children (forty or so children, one other adult testing with me, and even she is clearly younger than me by far) and not feel foolish. I see the parents of all the kids watching through their smartphones. I recognize how much I stand out when I get up to demonstrate my technique.

But tonight, doing my poomsae, there were all the black belts watching me, Master Hong, Master Kim, and of course Master Lee and that sea of children and parents.

I got up and thought only of the first move of the poomsae. Then the next move, then the next.

Tonight I earned a yellow belt with a green stripe. But something so much more has happened to me, and I'm ready to start giving even more.

But, only one kick, one punch, and one move at a time.

No mind.

DAVID IANETTA

LIVE WITHOUT LIMITS

I have often heard and sometimes repeated the well-known saying "youth is wasted on the young," but I don't believe that is a reflection on the young anymore.

I think that is an older person's way of resigning themselves to the limits age has placed on them. Basically feeling that the young are not conscious of the opportunities they have that the old would like to take advantage of but can't anymore.

Taekwondo has been teaching me that I do not know my limits unless I test them and the worst that can happen is I fail. Now the advantage of age is having the confidence to try that only comes with years of experience. There is also the freedom from being self-conscious of what others may think of us.

In light of that, I wanted to share two milestones that happened to me recently.

First, it is estimated that 75 percent of new TKD students will quit within six months of beginning training. Then, only one in ten will persist until reaching the rank of black belt.

I have made it through my ninth month of Taekwondo. According to statistics, I am now in the 25% of those who continue to train!

I have made it past that first hurdle. Since only one out of four gets as far as I have, I am confident that I will also be in the ten percent that make it to their black belt! I know that I will continue to grow and pursue my goal. To "focus on my goals" and "always finish what I start" are two TKD student commitments that stand out to me in regard to this.

The reward of my persistence is that my body is feeling stronger. I can especially see this in my legs. My kicks are getting stronger and better. I'm more flexible than I was before, all good signs that my body is adjusting to the training.

In fact, the other day I was kneeling down and I comfortably laid back, all the way until my back was on the ground, stretching my thighs! In class I was only inches away from touching my toes when master Hong came by and pushed down on my back causing me to make contact with them. Only a brief moment, but it felt like such a victory!

I never thought I would get this kind of flexibility back.

Another event was this weekend's tournament. I competed in the Raleigh Open Taekwondo Championship. I decided I was not ready for sparring, but went with Poomsae. Even though my one and only other tournament was over 30 years ago, I decided to give it a go.

It was not so much about coming home with a trophy, but to have the focused training on my Poomsae, and to push myself a little.

I actually won first place!

Now in light of full disclosure, there were only three of us in my rank and age group. However, the other two men were both younger than me and held higher belts.

But better than the trophy was the heartfelt congratulations of some of my classmates at my accomplishment. That was unexpected and to be honest, rather touching.

So, still going strong! Blue and yellow tips on my high yellow belt so next month I should be testing for my green belt!

Until then, stay healthy and never give up on your dreams.

DAVID IANETTA

TRAVELING BACK IN TIME

The older we get, the more we feel we cannot turn back the clock. Time, in some ways, has become our nemesis. Especially when you mix in regret. It is rare we can correct a bad choice or redeem a lost moment in time.

But tonight was an exception to that rule.

In a small way, I feel as if I walked back in time and got a high five from my 16-year-old self. I felt a timeless nod of respect from the young man I once was.

In Tang Soo Do there were only three belt changes. Green followed the white, red then black (midnight blue, actually).

As a teenager I worked twelve long months, from 10th gup (rank) to 6th to finally get a color belt. I remember after about ten months someone said to me, "You have been taking karate for almost a year and you have a white belt? Don't they give you that with the uniform?"

So, yeah, that green belt was well earned. And the feeling, to finally wrap an actual color around my waist, was amazing! I still remember it.

As the years passed, I have had to acknowledge that most of my technique was gone. If I ever entered a class again I could not put on the red or even green belt I had earned.

My level was lost. And somehow I knew I had let that young man inside me down.

But after tonight, I have that belt in my hands again. Ten months of training and I feel as if I went back in time and took hold of that dream once more.

It is, seriously, never too late to go back and rekindle a dream. No matter what that dream was. Don't look at what you have lost; work with what you have now.

The test also pushed my limits, as I think Master Kim likes to challenge me!

When it came time for breaking the boards, my first technique was a punch. Not too hard, I reasoned. A young black belt held one board in front of me and I felt ready to go.

Then at the last moment, Master Kim shouted to him to add two more.

Three boards!

The look on the young man's face was classic. He was amazed I would be asked to break three boards. He said something like, "can you break three?" to me. I smiled and said, "I guess we'll see..." The whole time I'm trying hard not to picture myself in the emergency room with a broken hand.

I focused as I had learned. Then I pushed away any doubt and simply punched through the three boards!

It was an amazing experience.

Then came time for the back kick. This one I had worried about. We never break boards in class, only in tests. I wasn't sure my technique was good enough.

To do a turning back kick you have to turn around, look over your shoulder at the target and then kick backwards. One board should break if you make any contact at all. There is a lot of strength in this kick.

But once again I was given three! And after the spectators saw me break three boards with a punch, I could feel all eyes on me as I stared at those three boards.

I knew the only thing for me to do was to go for it. Maybe I'd kick wrong and hurt my foot. Maybe I'd just bounce of the boards and have to do it again and again.

I pushed those thoughts away, along with the look of concern on the young black belt's face as he held the boards, and simply kicked.

All three boards broke and the room erupted into applause. It felt amazing.

I finished the test and went home with a green belt tied around my waist.

To me, the Green belt signifies reclaiming part of my heart. I keep thinking more about testing my limits, pushing my boundaries, taking more risks simply to see what I'm made of.

Getting this belt back is a turning point inside of me. It is propelling me to work harder and dream bigger.

What is your dream? Isn't it time you met up with that person inside you, looked them in the eyes and said, "yeah… let's do this!"

DAVID IANETTA

ONE YEAR IN, STILL GOING STRONG!

It's the beginning of summer, so this evening's class only has five students. Most of the students, teenagers, are studying for high school finals.

I don't mind this at all. Smaller classes mean more work. When we do exercises like lining up for kick drills, fewer of us in line means your turn comes up more frequently.

On this particular drill, Master Hong is holding a large padded target for me to practice roundhouse kicks on. I kick with my left foot, bounce a few times while he steps back and swaps sides, then kick with my right foot.

We do this up and down the Do Jang.

I remember back when I first started training. I tried to throw a roundhouse kick and could not.

To quote from my blog on July 1, 2015, "Last night we went over the roundhouse kick. I am shocked how much I have lost in 30 years. No matter how hard I tried, I could not execute this kick correctly. My legs flopped around with little to no focus. This is the first time I had to fight some discouragement."

Now I'm hitting the target, hard, with both legs.

It's been a year this month. I can't believe I've been taking Taekwondo consistently for a year and last night I just earned my high green belt!

There are four levels in Taekwondo. Level one consists of white belt and high white belt. Level two consists of yellow belt, high yellow, green and high green belt. So now I am at the top of level two.

Fitness and flexibility have been improving. I'm rather surprised at how much has come back.
But it doesn't feel like enough, not nearly enough.

After a year, basically 1/3 of the way to my black belt, I feel more motivated than ever.
They say it's good to write out goals. So some of my goals for this next year of TKD are as follows.

1 Increase endurance: My biggest struggle these days is getting out of breath too easily. My wind gives out before anything else does. In sparring, this is tough because only a few minutes into the match I'm sucking wind. I have a heavy bag, I need to start using it on weekends.

2 Increase flexibility: Stretching more, all the time. Especially at work and in the evenings.

3 Concentrate on basic technique and stances: Lock in my stances better and more consistently and learn the Korean terminology as I work out, so that it's second nature.

4 Focusing on tension in my body: Remaining relaxed in my blocks, strikes and kicks until the last part of the movement when the power is actually needed.

If all goes well, by this time next year I should be a deputy black belt. That is a belt that is half red and half black. The student stays on that belt for the next year as he works toward the black belt.

So I'm fixing my eyes on that black and red belt!

Bruce Lee once said, "If you spend too much time thinking about a thing, you'll never get it done." I spent years thinking about returning to Martial Arts, I can't stress enough how glad I am that I went beyond wishful thinking and actually did something about it. Lord willing, I will continue onto my black belt goal and beyond.

My wife has a motorcycle helmet that says, "No Limits" on it. Excuses place limits on following our dreams. That's why I have never researched just how much my fifty-one year old body can handle, I don't want the internet to tell me what I can and cannot do because I know I'll create excuses and limits from there.

So how about you? What have you put off that you should begin working toward? As you read through this blog, what comes to mind?

If my journey proves anything, it's that is never too late to begin pursuing a dream.

DAVID IANETTA

SAYING GOODBYE TO TANG SOO DO

After having studied Taekwondo for a year now, the original uniform top I purchased has worn rather thin. So thin, in fact, that the collar tore.

So to replace it, I purchased a traditional style top, like the one I wore when I took Tang Soo Do. I found it online and liked the style because it reminded me of the one I used to wear over 30 years ago.

When it arrived, the fabric seemed a little heavy, but I figured I'd give it a try in class. After all, there are students who just wear a t-shirt, so perhaps this top would be acceptable. Only one way to find out!

I arrived a few minutes early, as I normally do, and asked Master Hong, if the top was ok. He seemed to have a puzzled expression as he motioned to Master Lee and said to ask her.

I have to admit, until that moment, I didn't see anything that was all that different about my new top. Although I was getting a little hot… is it really hot in here? I wondered.

I found Master Lee and waited to ask her. By now I'm beginning to think, "it feels strange, being the only one who has a top like this" I felt like the guy who shows up dressed like a pirate, only to find out it wasn't a costume party.

I asked Master Lee about the top. After she stifled a laugh, she said, "Um… oh… that's a Judo top, Mr. David!" The statement itself contained the answer to my question!

Wrong style and, um… wrong country!

I could already feel the sweat beading on my body from the thick material. Although no one seemed to notice, when she said, "Judo top," I felt as if the whole dojang stopped moving and stared right at me, horrified. It was like that dream when you are standing in lunch line at school and realize you forgot to wear pants.

I had a quick mental fantasy of being surrounded by students chanting "Judo top, Judo top, Judo top!"

Judo, a Japanese art, requires a top with thicker material as you are often grabbed by the uniform and thrown around like a rag doll.

Now, the main style difference between a Taekwondo top and the one I had on is the TDK one is a pullover with a V-neck collar. This style is only found in TKD; it was introduced by the Kukkiwon in 1978. Some say it has earlier origins than that.

The one I was wearing was a cross over like a bathrobe. That was what I wore in Tang Soo Do (although much thinner material). There were other differences as well, such as the black belt was not black, but dark blue, etc.

Both Master Hong and Master Lee acted like it was no big deal and the other students never noticed.

But I kept thinking about it. How could I not see the drastic difference between how I looked and how the other students looked until that moment?

And then it dawned on me. I was holding onto the past. I was seeing this experience through the eyes of something that was long gone.

Much like parents who try to have their child put their old regrets right; I was imposing the Tang Soo Do experience on top of this one.

Now I can see the evidence of it all the time. The difficulty in using the walking stance, the trouble with wanting to pull back my toes and strike with the ball of my foot, and even calling basic 1 (Taegeuk Il Jang) by the Tang Soo Do form name (Ki Cho Hyung IL BU).

Tang Soo Do gave me so much as a teenager. Not the least, two amazing friends who I am still in contact with today. But I have been seeing Taekwondo as an extension of the journey I walked away from so many years ago. I have been trying to pick up where I left off. Trying to somehow merge the two experiences, as if I were capable of going back in time. Like studying Taekwondo now, erases walking away from Tang Soo Do all those years ago.

Without realizing it, instead of seeing my progress in this new journey and being encouraged by it, I have seen myself as far behind where I once was. I was working from a deficit, instead of truly starting over from step one.

It's time to forget what is behind me and embrace today. To fold that old style uniform and leave it in a drawer of memories.

Today truly is a new day.

DAVID IANETTA

> "THERE ARE NO LIMITS. THERE ARE ONLY PLATEAUS... YOU MUST GO BEYOND THEM."
> - BRUCE LEE

Recently, we've had some hot, humid, weather and with it, thunder storms.

One of those nights, Master Hong, greeted me and then asked, "Mister David… how are your knees?"

"My knees, sir? They're OK"

"With this weather, they don't bother you at all do they? You can move OK tonight?"

"Oh, yes, sir I'm fine," I said, still sitting on the floor stretching out before class.

"Very good, sir," he said, and then said something to Master Ko in Korean.

At the end of that class, after the sheer amount of kicks and stretches we did, I replayed that conversation in my head.

This time I could read between the lines.

"Mister David… how are your knees?"

"My knees, sir? They're OK"

"With this weather, they don't bother you at all, do they? You can move OK? Because tonight I am going to push you to the utter limits of what you feel you can endure alongside all these much younger students."

"Oh, yes sir, I'm fine…" I said, still sitting on the floor stretching out before class.

"Very good, sir, because I'd hate to have you start out this class already in pain," he said, then said to Master Ko in Korean, "Yes we can do the ultra-difficult kicking and stretching drills tonight, Mister David will hopefully survive!"

There are some nights at Taekwondo when I truly feel my age, and I cannot help but feel a little envious of the young adults with their unlimited supply of energy and endurance. So many times when we start class with jogging around the dojang, I see some of them politely passing me.

Again, and again…

It was time to work on that endurance… among other things!

I had been talking about doing a good workout on Saturdays. I have my personal dojang in the backyard, with a heavy bag, mirror, and plenty of space to work out in.

So these past few weekends, I buckled down and went out there and did it!

It has felt great to add this additional workout.

One of my greatest challenges is still my endurance, so I really want to push myself in that area. Last class I sparred and knew that I could do so much better if I just could focus more on the match and less on breathing.

And this ties into something I realized while reading about the life of Bruce Lee.

Now, here is a guy who was ripped and had great abs back in the seventies. You know, during a time when people heard the term "six-pack" and thought only of drinks? Before people cared what abs were and forced all us men to never go shirtless again, unless we can display the body of Adonis...

But Bruce Lee didn't work out to get great abs. His focus was not on looking fit; it was on fitness itself.

Everything he did physically was with that in mind. The ripped body was just a by-product.

This has inspired me to focus more on fitness. I judge how effective my workouts have been, not by how I look, but on how I perform. Now this is a very different approach, and it sounds rather simple; but it was a bit of a revelation to me.

Progress can be slow sometimes, but it is indeed progress. Last class, Master Hong commented on my fitness after three sparring matches. He said that I had come a long way from where I started.

I don't always see the day-to-day progress, but I will keep striving to push myself by training harder and smarter.

So, still learning and growing in Taekwondo, but also learning about my body (and life) in general.

As I tell my wife, jokingly, before I leave for each class, "I'll be back just a little bit more badass..." to which she often replies, "I certainly hope so!"

Yes, I certainly do too!

DAVID IANETTA

TAKING IT UP A NOTCH WITH NUNCHAKUS AND SATURDAY WORKOUTS.

One of the advantages of taking Taekwondo at an older age is that I pay much more attention to my body than I did as a teenager.

When I was younger, I took for granted that my body would simply move as it needed to. I hadn't realized that the years of riding a bicycle combined with the strength and stamina of youth, gave me the strength needed for martial arts. When energy abounds, you don't need to conserve it.

So, fast-forward thirty years… As a fifty-one-year-old man, I have become much more "body conscious" as I strive to gain strength, flexibility, and better form.

My Saturday workout includes three core activities involving my whole body; activities that help me move toward those goals.

Number one: Keep my body relaxed, remove tension.

Practicing nunchakus are a great aid in this! When I was younger, that was my weapon of choice. My brother Steven gave me my first pair when I was fifteen.

Back then I noticed that the use of nunchakus developed my left side coordination. Basically working nunchakus evenly with both hands made my left kick coordination improve.

I am becoming more and more aware of how much I tense my body when I practice sparring, or even practice poomsae. Wasting energy on body tension quickly leads to fatigue (and often a comment from Master Hong, such as, "Mr. David, are you dizzy, do you need to sit down?")

Nunchakus are a great solution for the problem of body tension. I keep them constantly in motion while my mind focuses on relaxing my entire body. I have even found that the more relaxed I get, the faster they move.

And come on, let's face it -nunchakus are badass! Maybe I won't get a part in a cool Kung Fu flick, but I can feel like I am in one!

Until I drop them, that is. Yeah, I got to work on that.

I also focus on relaxing my body when doing heavy bag work. I do this by bouncing, while keeping my body relaxed. Then I kick and go right back to bouncing and relaxing.

The result is, I last longer.

Number two: Stretching all the time.

Seriously, all the time!

I stretch before, during, and especially after the workout. I am becoming more and more aware of the muscle groups that are affected when I kick. So I constantly stretch those muscles.

It has taken some time, but the flexibility is returning, my kicks are starting to look like they should.

Number three: Leg strength.

I have three basic exercises I do for this. First, I just put my leg in position by bringing my knee up and holding it there. I do this for the front kick, sidekick and roundhouse kick.

Next, I do the actual kicks, using a combination of the mirror and the heavy bag.

After that, I'm on the floor (an exercise I learned in class from Master Hong,) raising the leg in the roundhouse, and sidekick positions. I can feel the muscles burn when I do this, and boy do they burn!

Conditioning is a huge part of Taekwondo. And, of course, the by-product of all this work is a healthier and fit body.

Saturday's workouts are simple in that I focus on the basics. As my body becomes more fit, I'll add more to the workout.

Even though the temperatures have been in the high nineties, I have been constant for four Saturdays in a row. It's been hard, but very satisfying.

The best part is, I love it! Focusing on improving Taekwondo, I don't even notice the exercise I'm getting.

At times, I even feel young again.

DAVID IANETTA

REALITY CHECK: I'M A 51 YEAR OLD MAN TAKING TAEKWONDO WITH A BUNCH OF TEENAGERS.

The other night I came home from class still a little winded from the sparring sessions. We had three 2-minute sessions back to back after 30 minutes of warm-ups and kicking exercises.

I hobbled up the stairs, stripped off my sweaty uniform and took a nice hot shower. Then I went back down the stairs and made an "old man" grunt noise when I sat down in my chair.

My breathing became regular and my heart rate slowed to a normal pace. But muscle fatigue was setting in. It was a hard workout, a good one, but a hard one.

And I was feeling my age.

I stood there shaking my head and thinking, "I'm a 51-year-old man taking Taekwondo with a bunch of teenagers."

But then I got up from my chair, and sat on the floor. I knew I had to stretch my rebelling muscles into moving again, and another thought came into my mind.

"I'm a 51-year-old man taking TKD with a bunch of teenagers!!"

The same truth can be looked at in two different ways.

I could focus on the negative while training. Being in a class with mostly teenagers (who have an abundance of energy, stamina, and flexibility) could cause me to fall short in comparison.

Breaking a board with a spinning hook.
After all, they kick higher, move faster and never seem to get winded. One would think my breathing like Darth Vader during a sparring match would intimidate them, but it unusually just generates a look of concern.

"Are you ok Mr. David… do you need to sit down?"

I could stay with this unrealistic comparison. I could allow it to discourage me.

Sometimes I do, sometimes I focus too much on my failures (more on that later,) what I cannot do (yet,) not what I am capable of doing now.

But that is not the whole picture is it?

I am a 51-year-old in a class with a bunch of teenagers and I'm keeping up with them.

Focusing too much on where we want to be can easily stop us from enjoying where we are.

Last night I tested for, and earned, my blue belt. I am now at level three.

To review, level one is white and high white, level two is yellow to high green (four belts,) level three is blue to high red (four belts,) and level four is deputy black and black belt.

I learned two lessons about myself from this test last night.

First it is hard for me to shake off a mistake and keep going strong.

When performing Taeguk Sah Jang (poomsae 4,) I made a single mistake. Out of 18 steps, I did one block with the wrong arm.

After being told what I did wrong, I was asked to repeat the poomsae. As I did, I had trouble shaking off the embarrassment of making that mistake. Each step I executed was affected by the negative thoughts. When I came to that point again, I made the same mistake and was gently corrected by Master Kim.

So lesson one, get rid of pride. Everyone makes mistakes, I have to accept that I am human and learn from them.

The other lesson was how often the thing you dread turns out to be nothing. What I worried the most about this test was being able to hit and break a board with a spinning hook kick. I practiced all I could, but hitting a heavy bag is not the same as hitting a small target accurately and with enough force to break a board.

When the time came, I was first asked to break four boards with a punch. This was fun and my confidence was back up. Then came time to break the board with the spinning hook kick. It's hard to watch myself with this kick in the mirror because of the very nature of it. I'm spinning around (and trying not to get dizzy,) so I always felt it was sloppy and not accurate, even after Master Hong did target kicking drills with us this past week.

Yet when it came time to execute the kick, I did it smoothly and without any effort broke the board on the first attempt. Reviewing the video, it doesn't look sloppy at all.

So, again, the lesson of not borrowing grief, not worrying about things that often come to nothing.

I'm at level three now! Time to dig in and keep going. I've learned so much since that first class over a year ago. I'm having the time of my life here, just goes to prove, it is never too late to follow your passions.

DAVID IANETTA

FINALLY IN THE RED!

I've been seeing red for a long time now, ever since the first day when I put on that bleached white belt and started this journey toward my black belt.

All the belts, from white to black are displayed, in order, on a wall in the dojang.

I know this because I'm normally early for class. I watch the advanced class before mine as they finish up; I always look at those belts.

I see where the belt I was currently wearing falls in that progression. I see how far I have come, and also how far I have still to go.

And during those times, I always look at the red in the higher belts.

In the beginning, the red seemed a very long way off. It was that same feeling I get when I set off on a long car trip, realizing I have only driven a few miles out of hundreds.

This past week I tested for and received my High Blue belt. This is a blue belt with a red stripe. The next belt is solid red, and the high red belt is red with a white stripe.

After that comes the deputy black belt, a belt that is half red and half black. The common color in all these higher levels is the red.

Red belt was the last rank I received in Tang Soo Do.

I'm not sure whatever happened to that original belt. I just know that at some point in my life I realized I couldn't wear it anymore. I had lost so much of my technique it would almost be a mockery to put it back on.

But know, I have worked hard to have that red in my belt again. Seeing the red stripe tells me that I made a choice over a year and a half ago that has led me to this current accomplishment.

I've made it this far, I'm finally in red.

There is a lot to be said for living in the now, but there is also much to be said about the choices we make now, shaping our future.

For example, four years ago, a doctor told me I was pre-diabetic. I was basically looking at a life of living with diabetes. I slowly made changes to my diet, and added the regular exercise of Taekwondo. On my last physical, my sugar numbers were totally normal.

I changed my health with a series of choices. Diabetes is not a part of my life today because of choices I made in the past.

At every test, Master Kim asks several students what their long-term and short-term goals are. It's easier not to put goals that are way out there, so you don't have to deal with not accomplishing them. Like those of us who have given up on New Year's resolutions know... After a while the pain of failure stomps the desire to try out of us.

But though a life of not trying may seem safe, is that really living?

One of the advantages of getting older is realizing that time goes by very fast. Looking at a three-year goal to get my black belt doesn't seem nearly as daunting at is did when I was a kid. Armed with the knowledge of how fast the years pass, I now to take on other long term goals.

You know, the kind of goals that take time to achieve, ones that take years to get any good at.

But I am at peace with the process. I know now that, just as sure as time marches on, I will slowly work toward achieving them.

Youth has physical stamina, but with age comes a mental discipline that gives us that edge.

What about you? What have you put off because it seemed impossible or would take too long? What choice can you make now, today, that you will be happy you did a year from now?

Grabbing ahold of this new belt, and moving forward, one kick and one step at a time.

DAVID IANETTA

FANNING THE FLAME OF DESIRE

When I learn a new poomsae, I always go to YouTube where all the forms can easily be found. Although you can't learn Taekwondo online, it can be a great asset for remembering techniques and poomsae.

The other day I was watching the Taeguk Yuk Jang form and trying to commit the new moves to memory for practice later.

As I looked at the black belt demonstrating the poomsae, I found myself just staring at his black-trimmed uniform and belt. Suddenly I became aware of just how much I wanted that black belt around my waist.

The strong desire was there, and as I watched him perform each move, it was like fanning the flames of a fire. I wanted to get better, and I want to earn that black belt.

Only 10% of the people who start this journey make it to the black belt level.

After Christmas break, I wondered if that first class back would have Master Hong taking it easy on us or pushing us harder? First class back also corresponded with my first day back to work after four days off. I was amazed at how fast the "lazy" can settle in, even during such a short amount of time. Part of me wanted to skip practice, but the other part of me knew (maybe the older and perhaps a little wiser part?) that the longer I waited, the harder it would be for me to go back.

So with that in mind, I suited up, left the house, again wondering… easy class tonight or hard?

It turned out to be the latter.

Master Hong had two visiting masters from South Korea helping with the class. Master Kwan and Master Han will be here for two months. Along with the new instructors there were perhaps fifteen students. This was comprised of mostly black belts, a few deputy black belts and me.

I looked around at the advanced students and extra instructors and I knew I was in for a great class.

Right from the start we worked very hard. Throwing kick after kick, moving forward in front stances and changing different blocks until my legs felt like they would collapse.

I was quickly covered in sweat and a few times had to catch my breath.

And, of course, Master Hong checked in on me from time to time.

"Are you OK Mr. David?"

"Don't run so fast Mr. David!"

Toward the end of class, one of the visiting masters assisted me with my poomsae. Although new to English, she communicated "NO!" rather well when I did something wrong, with a very stern expression on her young face. But she also flashed a bright smile when I got it right.

This young woman personified my approach to Taekwondo beautifully – take it seriously, but keep your heart light.

The class was hard, but at the end I felt amazing! And, needless to say, I slept very well that night.

Better than I did even while on break for the holidays.

My passion for TDK felt rejuvenated.

It was in this frame of mind that I watched the YouTube video and felt that longing to see this journey through to that black belt and beyond.

I want to earn that belt, I'm not giving up.

Sometimes it's hard to pursue something we are passionate about, but nothing truly worthwhile comes easily, and often we have to pay some kind of price.

Yet, in the end, that's what makes obtaining the prize all the sweeter.

DAVID IANETTA

CAUGHT UP WITH THE PAST, NOW PUSHING TO THE FUTURE

It's the morning of testing day and my eyes slowly adjust to the pitch-black bedroom. I know that it's early still, and since it's Saturday I can sleep in. I turn toward the alarm and see it is 5:00 AM.

Plenty of time to sleep!

At 5:22 I am still doing my poomsae in my head. There is one move I'm not completely sure of. In my mind, I repeat the poomsae over and over again.

The test isn't for another six hours, but now I'm wide-awake. No matter how much I try to shut my brain off and go back to sleep, I know as each minute ticks by, it's pointless to try.

I get up, and head downstairs as quietly as I can. In the silence of my living room I go over the poomsae again. Then I check YouTube and reassure myself that, yes I had it right all along.

I'm pretty comfortable with public speaking, and I actually enjoy playing guitar and signing in front of a crowd. However, there is something about testing day that still makes me nervous.

When I get to the Dojang, I'm reassured as another adult student confides in me that even after time spent in the military, testing makes her very nervous as well. Ok, it's not just me!

My nerves began to settle a little bit as the test got underway. When it was my turn to come up I remembered my poomsae and my kicking techniques.

Next came breaking and sparring both of which I enjoy, especially the board breaking.

When I broke three boards with a punch, it was rather dramatic. The boards are not very thick, so when I punched them, I basically hit the middle out of them, which caused the boards to break into nine pieces instead of six, scattering pieces all about!

I always find the younger students' reactions to my board-breaking amusing. After this test, one young boy told me with much enthusiasm, how I needed to be in a tournament because I always break "like, fifteen boards!"

It might be impressive to the little kids, but I know what is truly worthy of that kind of admiration.

We took a short break during the test and we had two visiting masters demonstrate poomsae. This was a huge treat!

Master Kwon and Master An are both South Korean world champions and amazing to watch. Seeing them demonstrate is seeing Taekwondo on a whole different level. I am both inspired and challenged by their expertise. It is very much a privilege to have them help with the instruction during class.

The testing finally over, my name was called and I was handed my belt.

It is almost a surreal feeling putting this belt on. This was the highest belt I earned in Tang Soo Do over thirty-five years ago. The same belt I took off one day when I turned my back on something I loved. Putting it back on is a very symbolic reminder to me that I truly have picked up this journey again.

Life doesn't always give us second chances to finish something we gave up on.

I write this book for myself, to document my journey. But for those of you who are reading along, it is my sincere hope that you can gain some inspiration and return to whatever passion you may have walked away from.

If a fifty-something-year old man can take up Taekwondo, anything is possible!

DAVID IANETTA

BE WATER, MY FRIEND.

It was another very brutal class. After almost 35 minutes of non-stop moving, including obstacle courses (two hops in, one hop backwards, faster and faster) and target kicking, it was time to fully gear up and spar.

First I faced a young black belt who Master Hong nicknamed "Bruce Lee" because he does look somewhat like the young Bruce Lee did. He took it easy on me and was very encouraging, but by now I was winded.

Next I stood toe-to-toe with Mister M. He's a man closer to my age, with a great joyful spirit. One look at him told me he was now just as exhausted as I was. We circled each other like Rocky and Apollo at the end of Rocky II. Remember that scene? Their eyes are almost completely swollen shut after fifteen rounds of pounding one another, shuffle stepping, just wanting it over.

That's just how I felt, I fully expected us to fall down at the same time, in slow motion.

Anyway, we were both taking it very easy on each other; both hoping the match would end soon. I had nothing left, huffing and puffing.

But it was comical and we both laughed.

Master Hong approached, smiled and said, "Yes, you are both tired, it's ok, go easy… go easy…"

At the end Mister M and I shook hands and laughed again. Then he said something that will stick with me for a long time.

"I don't compare myself with the young people in this class, but with the men our age who aren't here. To where I would be physically if I wasn't here."

Good point!

That leads me to something that has been nagging at the back of my mind. I wonder why I still get out of breath when I spar?

The answer came with my last physical. I found out that I have a "floppy valve" in my heart and need to see a specialist. My regular doctor couldn't tell me anything about the condition. So I'm in a waiting mode.

What will the specialist say? Will I just have to live with this? Will it get worse?

The thought of this "out of breath problem while sparring" never going away, had me down for a little while.

But as I wait to get more information, I've come to a conclusion that I will stick with no matter the results.

One of the tenets of taekwondo is to develop an indomitable spirit. Essentially, never giving up.

Sure, at first I was disheartened, but then I thought, "What can I do? If this never goes away, what am I still capable of doing?"

I can get more flexible and I can get stronger. I can focus on poomsae and technique, making every kick, block and stance better and better. I can get my Korean terminology where it should be.

As for sparring, I figure I will just have to adapt. I will save my "wind," work on being faster with more accurate kicks and learn to breathe better when struck. I will develop combinations that are fast and efficient.

So with this current physical challenge, I know no matter the outcome, I'll still be kicking!

I guess it's time to take Bruce Lee's words to heart, so I'll close with this very well-known quote.

"Empty your mind, be formless. Shapeless, like water. If you put water into a cup, it becomes the cup. You put water into a bottle and it becomes the bottle. You put it in a teapot, it becomes the teapot. Now, water can flow or it can crash. Be water, my friend."

DAVID IANETTA

MORE EFFORT = BETTER RESULTS

Weekend workouts are starting to pay off!

Maybe it's because of my age, or maybe it's because of a busy life, but one of the toughest things for me to do has been remembering my poomsae.

Poomsae is a series of anywhere from 18 to 22 moves, performed in a pattern that basically simulates fighting multiple assailants attacking from many directions.

In taekwondo they are pretty important.

So what happens is, I work on one for a few months and get it ready for testing day. But after the test comes and goes, the memory of the sequence of moves fades away. Especially as I learn the next one.

This has been stressing me out a bit. I know that when I test for my black belt, I'm going to have to perform them all.

It's not enough for me to remember the movements; I want to execute them well. I want to have a strong technique.

My solution? Being consistent with my weekend workouts.

I've been at this now for about a month and they are finally starting to pay off!

I do Taegeuk Yuk Jang (my previous poomsae) eight times. Next I do Taegeuk Oh Jang eight times as well, for a total of sixteen times

There are a total of eight Taegeuk poomsae. My thought is, I will eventually be doing each one twice for a total of sixteen times.

The result of this effort has been that I am remembering both forms!

As for the ones I already learned and have forgotten, they will be repeated again when I get my deputy black belt and work toward my black belt.

Remembering the movements is not the only benefit of this extra practice time.

The other night in class, I went over Taegeuk Oh Jan for about twenty minutes with Master Ko. Because I already knew the movements, he was able to focus on refining my technique.

Even Master Lee came by and gave me pointers to have better technique.

So by putting forth the effort on the weekends, I'm getting more out of the class time. This, in turn, makes me want to put in more effort on the weekends.

I also work on kicking. After my body has been amply warmed up, first with nunchakus to get the blood flowing, then stretching and poomsae, I go into my personal dojang for kick training. Most of this is bag work.

As my legs begin to get tired, I alternate with sit-ups and some light weight training.

All in all, a great workout! I've passed the point of the, "I have to do this" and now look forward to my training time. My enthusiasm is up, I'm enjoying myself and I'm seeing some results.

DAVID IANETTA

"THERE'S A LION ON THE ROAD! YES, I'M SURE THERE'S A LION OUT THERE!"

My body is covered in sweat as I sit down on the floor in my personal dojang. Slowly I bend into a stretch, feeling my hamstring beginning to protest. I ignore its cries for mercy and lean a little more into the stretch.

I slowly count to ten and then relax my leg. Now I give the other leg its fair share of abuse.

One, two, three, four, five, six, seven, eight, nine… ten.

Next I grab the ball of my foot, I slowly extend my leg upwards and accomplish something I have not been able to do since I began taekwondo over a year and a half ago.

My leg extends, completely, as my knees locks in place. I sit there astonished.

Did I actually just do that?

What may seem small is a major breakthrough for me. I have proven to myself that I can get my flexibility back. My daily stretching is paying off.

And to think I almost skipped this monumental workout because it was cold and rainy outside.

It all started with my wife's morning walk.

Even though it was raining and cold, she was determined to get out there. As she was out walking, I was inside the house, mourning the foul weather. My do jang has no heat; it would be cold and damp in there. My body is too old to risk tensing up working out in the cold. I had about a half a dozen other excuses running through my mind, as I was about to skip my Saturday workout.

When Rika came back in from her walk, I commented on how I admire the fact that she went out in the rain. Then she said something that echoed in my mind for the next hour or so. She told me, "I'm determined to walk every day, if I start making excuses as to why I can't, soon I'll be out of the habit."

So here is my wife, out walking in the rain, and me practically whining that my dojang will be cold and feel damp. Although she didn't purposely set out to challenge me, I couldn't ignore the obvious.

I needed to man up!

Seriously, a grown man not wanting to work out because it's a little cold and damp?

I suddenly had an image of Cain in Kung Fu, grasping the hot cauldron. As it burns a tiger and dragon into his forearms, he looks up at me and says, "Really? And you want to call yourself a martial artist?"

I went out the dojang, wearing a flannel shirt over my tank top. Within minutes, I had to strip that off. The more I moved, the warmer I felt. I worked the bag then I practiced my tornado kick. I worked my left leg roundhouse kick (a weak point,) and stopped to stretch throughout the whole hour. I worked on my poomsae.

A few weeks ago, Master Hong pointed out that my front stance was too deep, so to break that habit I came up with tying a rope around my ankles, forcing my stance to be only two shoulder widths wide as it should be.

As I finished my workout with stretching and reached that milestone, I thought about excuses and Proverbs 26:13 came to mind. This ancient book is over four thousand years old, yet it accurately described my attitude;

"The lazy person claims, "There's a lion on the road! Yes, I'm sure there's a lion out there!"

How many times to we stay inside and not embrace what we can do because we are simply too lazy? How many other milestones are out there, left unreached, because we allow ourselves to be our own worst enemy?

DAVID IANETTA

THIS IS TAEKWONDO!

Saturday, testing day for my high red belt.

There were only two other adults testing and they were matched up with each other for the sparring time. So when my name was called, I ran up to the mark and looked at the young man who I'd be sparring against.

Very young, I'd put him at maybe eleven years old.

He's a deputy black belt, and therefore not someone from my class (my class consists of teenagers and adults. When the command came to begin, I had already made my mind up to go easy on him.

That was my first mistake.

This young man came out kicking! He moved faster and kicked harder than his size first indicated. I found myself backing away, using an X-block over and over again to stop him from scoring.

When he did make contact, it was intense. Just goes to show, size really means nothing when it comes to Taekwondo.

For the first round, I struggled between wanting to do well against him, and hesitating to go all out because of his age and size.

Finally, I decided to give him back a little. After all, we were wearing protective gear; I could afford to get a few shots in. But I knew I had to engage soon, his youthful attack was wearing me out!

At one point he turned at me, leaving his chest fully exposed; instinctively I kicked.

And he was knocked to the ground and I felt terrible.

I offered him a hand up that he gladly took, smiling the whole time. Then we continued. Soon I forgot his age. His skill level and higher rank made up for that.

I'd like to say he held his own against me, but truthfully it was the other way around. Had they been keeping score, he would have been the victor.

I thought about Yoda, "Judge me by my size do you?"

At the end of the match we shook hands and he gave me a quick hug saying, "good job!"

As we went to sit down, I knew I had witnessed a young man who truly had an indomitable spirit. Later, as I was leaving the school, his father called over to me and said, "See you next time. I saw you today, you are very good!" I pointed to his son and said, "Thank you, so is he!"

The rest of my high red belt test went well. In fact, it went much better than any test before it. I attribute this to my weekend workouts. I was much more prepared.

Rather than just worrying about remembering my poomsae, I was focused on doing it well. Kicking techniques went off without a hitch.

For breaking, I had to break two boards with a tornado kick. Again, my weekend workouts assisted me, as I had been hitting the heavy bag with this kick. The seventeen-year-old black belt who held my boards, smiled widely and congratulated me when I executed the kick. The affirmation felt great. This kick was my greatest challenge until now. Being able to execute it correctly, with enough power to break two boards, was a big accomplishment for me.

I left the school with my high red belt.

Sunday came and I went out to my personal dojang to work out. I warmed up as normal with nunchakus, then did some stretching and moved right into poomsae.

It was around the seventh or eighth time going through Taegeuk Oh Jang that I came to a realization.

This is Taekwondo.

What I mean by that is, the pressure was off. I had tested with this poomsae and passed the test.

Yet here I was practicing it, over and over, for the simple pleasure of doing it. The two poomsae I have worked in to memory, Oh jang and Yuk Jang, are becoming a part of me. To neglect them would be to neglect my own body. I could not just kick back this Sunday; happy I had earned a new belt. I needed to spend time doing Teakwondo

It was a moment of clarity for me and I thought about it further as I was covered in sweat, stretching. I have crossed over a barrier; something inside me has changed, or perhaps grown stronger.

I began this journey as a white belt who had lost pretty much all he had learned over thirty years ago, but now, almost two years later, my body is stronger and more flexible. I stretch daily and I work out four times a week.

Looking at my high red belt with its white stripe, I realized that the familiar white in the belt signifies a new beginning for me.

Perhaps I truly am on my way to becoming a martial artist.

"If the martial arts practitioner concentrates on one basic technique a day, striving for complete perfection, he will, after even one year, have accumulated a wealth of techniques that no money can buy and no thief can steal. The individual does not have these qualities so much as he is them." – Sang Kyu Shim, "The making of a martial artist"

TWO YEARS IN, REACHING FOR MY
DEPUTY BLACK BELT PART 1

There are few things more discouraging than looking at an injury that has the potential of keeping you from your goal.

You work and you strive, often pushing past the pain. You discipline yourself to achieve your goal. And then, when it is within reach, something unexpected happens and sets you back.

I'm feeling that right now.

About a week ago I was in Taekwondo class and I injured my knee. I knew that night when I came home, that I had overdone things. I could barely walk after my shower.

Then to make matters worse, 36 hours after the injury, I was on a plane to Toronto for work. There was no time to treat it properly and let it heal. I did the best I could, but a day of traveling, (alternating between walking between gates and sitting uncomfortably on the planes) then teaching half a day standing up, only to wake the next morning and travel back, did a number on my knee. By the time I got home on Saturday, it was throbbing.

Ice, wrap with Ace bandage, repeat. That was my Sunday and Monday. Now it's Tuesday night and it is feeling somewhat better.

But, it gave out a few times today like those "trick knees" you hear about on TV. Just walking, I'd get taken off guard by a sharp pain.

I can't trust it right now, and that sucks.

Old man David, he has that trick knee, it gave out on him… he fell down and broke a hip. Need to chip in and get him an emergency alarm….

Sigh.

For months, in addition to my weekly classes, during the week, I've been waking up at five am to work out and work on poomsae. I know my form, I know my kicks, I'm ready for my test, scheduled for this week. This is a major step for me. I just passed my two-year mark and I will be testing for my Deputy Black Belt. That will make me a Level 4, and two-thirds the way to my Black Belt goal.

And right when it is in my grasp, I'm sitting here rubbing Tiger Balm on my knee and re-wrapping it with my trusted Ace Bandage. Hoping it will heal enough for me to test Friday night.

I went through a short bout of self-pity, my mind really wanted to go down that familiar path. But then I thought, what can I learn from this?

First, I can use this time as a reminder to work my body even more when it is feeling strong and uninjured. Stop being lazy at night and skipping my nightly stretches. Push a little more on the weekends to make my legs stronger.

I can also learn to listen to my body more. I knew, in class, that I was pushing beyond what my body could handle. I knew something was wrong. But I kept going anyway, I let pride get in the way of common sense.

Let's see what happens Friday night at my test.

"When life gives you obstacles, you must summon the courage and WALK ON." - Bruce Lee

"LESSONS WHILE WAITING"
DEPUTY BLACK BELT PART 2 OF 3

"Whether I like it or not, circumstances are thrust upon me, and being a fighter at heart, I sort of fight it in the beginning. But soon realize that what I need is not inner resistance and needless conflict, rather by joining forces to readjust, I need to make the best of it." - Bruce Lee

As I write this, my knee is still in an Ace bandage, and I have not yet tested for my deputy black belt.

Right up until the Friday of the exam, I had planned to push myself and test, no matter what. The sharp pain in my knee was gone and I felt I could at least limp through the test and get my belt.

But driving home from work that day, I experienced some sharp pain in my knee that I knew was my body's way of telling me I was crazy to even try. I stopped by the Do Jang and told Master Lee that I would not be able to test. She reassured me that I could test privately after my next class.

So I waited and I began to heal.

But as I slowly healed, I grew more impatient and restless. I wanted to get back to the Do Jang, I wanted to get my full workout in.

Finally I had a day where I could quickly ascend the stairs in my home without issue and I decided to go back to life as normal. Even though I still had a little tightness, I decided to ignore it.

Once again I twisted my knee, just a little, and the swelling returned.

Lesson one came through loud and clear. The body needs time to heal. You can aid it, but you cannot rush it. I had to fight a lot of discouragement at this time, but finally I began to try to exercise my mind some and at least do some reading.

My next lesson came in two parts.

I have been reading about Wu Wei. Wu Wei is the cultivation of a mental state in which our actions are quite effortlessly in alignment with the flow of life. I have always been baffled by something Bruce Lee said that he got from this system of thought.

He said, "I mean here is natural instinct and here is control. You are to combine the two in harmony. Not... if you have one to the extreme, you'll be very unscientific. If you have another to the extreme, you become, all of a sudden, a mechanical man... no longer a human being. So it is a successful combination of both, so therefore, it's not pure naturalness, or unnaturalness. The ideal is unnatural naturalness, or natural unnaturalness." (Emphasis mine.)

I thought about this statement and I kept coming back to the same questions in my mind, "How? Do I do this in any other area of my life? And if I do, how did I get there?"

Then it dawned on me, this is exactly what I do when I play guitar. At first when I was learning, it was very mechanical. Strumming and changing chords take work, effort and a lot of concentration.

But then, after time and much practice it is effortless. Now I don't think, I play. I have repeated the unnatural movements of playing until it somehow linked to my being in such a way as to transcend effort. It is unnatural naturalness. Playing guitar is pure instinct.

Explaining this to Rika, she said it sounded just like shifting gears on a motorcycle. We don't think about it, we do it.

And that lead me into realizing that I need to approach Taekwondo with this concept firmly fixed in my mind. I must repeat the movements over and over again, with a concentrated effort, until I achieve what I have in both riding a motorcycle and playing guitar. Until the unnatural movements become a natural part of my being.

Another part of this was realizing I could have used this time with my knee being out to practice my blocks and punches. I could have even sat on a stool and simply repeated them over and over to get the movements down. While one part of the body was recovering, I could have paid special attention to another.

I acted as if my whole body was incapable of Taekwondo simply because my knee is on the mend. Instead of feeling like I was losing time, I could have kept my forward momentum.

I feel with these lessons in mind, I will emerge from this time a better martial artist.

I know from experience that this approach to Taekwondo will flood into the rest of my life. There will be a part three to this blog when I return to class and finally test for my deputy black belt.

"If you truly love life, don't waste time because time is what life is made of." – Bruce Lee

"RETURN TO THE DO JANG"
DEPUTY BLACK BELT PART 3

I'm sitting on the bench waiting for the Level 4 (Black Belt and Deputy Black Belt) class to complete and I'm having doubts.

Am I ready to be back? What can I actually do? Will I be allowed to test tonight for my Deputy Black Belt?

It was hard not to stare up at that red and black belt on the wall.

I stretched some, rubbed my knee, and waited.

Master Lee saw me and smiled, "Welcome back!" she said giving me a hug. I asked her if I could test tonight and she said that Master Ko would evaluate me and see if I were ready.

I've been waiting almost two full months to come back. In that time, I've done a lot of reading. Reading about Bruce Lee's life, Wu Wei, and the many philosophies behind Martial Arts. I took two supplements, Omega 3 and Glucosamine, and I've slowly been exercising my knee back to health.

Waiting and reading...

I've done a few lighter workouts focusing on poomsae and

nunchakus. I even repaired a pair I have where the nylon cords had frayed.

And I waited on my body to recover.

It's been a rough road back; all the limping caused my back to have issues as well.

I've been hobbling around the office at work. I'm a bit over people asking me what's wrong with my leg. Some days I limp more than others, depending on how my back is feeling.

Even a store greeter smiled and said, "Did you hurt yourself?"

Ugh, am I ever going to heal from this? I know that in our fifties, we recover much slower, but wow, I never thought this would go on as long as it has.

Old man David, sigh.

This past Saturday, I spent an hour working out, going through my poomsae and stretching. I'm not completely healed; my knee is often tight and in need of more stretching. But there is no pain and it is slowly getting better each day. It seems to feel better with exercise, that to me was a sign that I can go back to class.

Class started and I was greeted with a smile and double high five from Master Ko and Master Won. They both seemed genuinely happy to see me back. I told them my knee was still recovering, and they encouraged me to take it very slowly.

For the opening stretches I did ok, not nearly like I normally could. Then when everyone else was jogging around the Dojang, I walked.

Don't run over Old Man David…

First I thankfully worked one-on-one with Master Won, just stretching. That was a welcome relief. She was very patient and careful with me.

Next I worked with her to do my poomsae. She asked me if I remembered and I told her I did. Master Won seemed genuinely surprised and pleased as I did the poomsae without forgetting a step. Kicking technique also went well.

She finished working with me and I was told to practice my kicking and poomsae by myself. I was careful not to push my knee.

When class finally ended I breathed a sigh of relief as Master Ko told me he would test me tonight. I remembered my poomsae and kicking technique effortlessly. Because my knee was still recovering, he waived the breaking and sparring requirements.

As Master Ko helped me put the belt on, and Master Won congratulated me, I felt elated.

Although I still have a long way to go in recovery, I am still on the road to get my black belt.

Now a level four, I have made it past the two-year point. My body doesn't always feel the strongest, but in my heart I'm still that 16-year-old, full of spirit and kicking high.

The journey continues!

HE TASKS ME...HE TASKS ME...

Wow, our bodies actually are changing as we get older… Huh…who'd have thought?

Healing is coming at a slow pace.

I cannot think of a time I have ever taken this long to recover from something! I won't accept limitations, I will continue to push my body to see what I am still capable of; but I will be realistic on how much work I need to do to keep my body in top shape.

I want to avoid injuries like this in the future. I wasn't careful, and my body was not strong enough or flexible enough to keep up with the teenagers around me. And it's so hard not to strive to "show them this old man has what it takes!"

Pride, it's a terrible thing.

The good news is, I do feel that my knee is getting stronger every day.

But man, I really want to kick that heavy bag! I feel like Khan in Star Trek 2, "He tasks me…" Of course Khan is quoting Ahab in Moby Dick, so do I feel like Khan, or Ahab? Sometimes I put way too much thought into these things.

Point is, I want to kick something solid!

Time, in time...

One very good thing that has come out of this injury is getting some great one-on-one training time with Master Won.

As I have said in earlier blogs, the evening class I attend is small, maybe about a dozen students at most. Almost all of them are black belts or deputy black belts.

Because my knee is still recovering, I'm not able to do the same drills that everyone else is doing. So while they are all sparring or kicking bags, I get to work with Master Won.

So far we have been working on refining my blocks. I really enjoy these sessions, as they are a chance to really improve my technique.

We do everything from proper hand position, (both in the starting position of the blocks and in the end) to how you get from point A to point B. It takes a lot of concentration to make sure that I do this correctly.

Also the blocks have to be executed in such a way that you stay relaxed for about 70 percent of the movement until you twist the wrist and snap that last 30 percent for power. I still struggle with tension in my upper body. Master Won is constantly putting her hands on my shoulders and pushing them down, telling me to relax.

Relaxing my body has proved to be very challenging. In martial arts, it's important to conserve your energy as much as possible. Tension in the body simply depletes that energy quicker.

And I know the only way to make these moves become second nature is to practice them, exactly as they should be, over and over.

I've learned something about my attention span while doing

this. I am easily distracted, a something that has developed from working in front of a computer all day. So the simple task of doing one thing and staying on that task with my mind and my body is rather challenging.

This makes me think about how I approach life.

How much energy do I deplete with tensions caused by worry or fear? How often does my mind wander far away from the present moment?

How often do I allow distractions to enter my mind?

Martial Arts are about so much more than just honing our bodies. If you pay close attention, you can really learn a lot about not only who you are, but also who you want to be.

DAVID IANETTA

50 SHADES OF PHYSICAL THERAPY

These days I find myself tied up with rubber bands, lunging onto equipment that has been made purposely to be unstable and working my muscles until they ache and beg me to stop. My ice bag has become my newest friend. Working through pain has been come a regular part of my life.

These past months have been the most physically challenging of my life. My knee injury and the lack of activity following it had a profound negative effect on my whole leg as well. To sum up what my Physical Therapist told me, the work I did to build my larger muscles put stress on the smaller supporting ones. The result was muscle fatigue and tightness. The injury was basically my legs screaming, "enough!"

The cure has been a concentrated effort of PT on flexibility in my hips and target strengthening of my knees and hip flexors.

Currently I still walk with a slight limp. I'm not free to do any twisting kicks or to kick any solid targets.

I've been back in class, where I modify the workout to my new requirements. On the nights I'm not in class, I do my PT exercises. I also do PT every morning. I ice my knee often.

This has been a huge exercise in patience! It is hard to stick with all this when only seeing the smallest hints of progress. There are days I wonder how much I will be able to recover. Sometimes at night, after class or a PT session I have to claw my way up the stairwell, hanging onto the railing and wall like some monster rising from a pit.

Did I leave my book downstairs? Crap, now I have to go down and come back up… again?

Progress has been slow, very slow. Only this week have I finally been able to lock my right knee out again so my leg is completely straight. So my legs are getting stronger, but slowly.

However, as the saying goes, "it was the best of times, it was the worst of times." There has been some good coming out of the last few months!

Recently I have joined forces with another man my age and this has added an awesome new dimension to my practice.

I have always respected Rick, a 3rd Dan Black belt from my school. His great attitude and indomitable spirit stands out to me in a sea of young people where I often find myself lost. Rick had come to symbolize to me that I can do it, I can make it and that I'm actually not crazy for trying.

Or maybe Rick is just as crazy as I am, but either way I enjoy his friendship.

Recently Rick has come to join me on Saturday mornings at my home Do Jang. This allows us to work on many of the aspects of Taekwondo that our school does not focus on.

And we work at a pace we can't always get in a class designed primarily for the young.

First there is extra stretching that people our age need. Rick introduced me to a form of stretching that combines isometric tension and stretching. The result is remarkable. We have both seen some progress with this in only a few short weeks.

We are also able to work on one step fighting. Basically one person throws a punch while the other works on countering with a predetermined set of movements. The benefit of these exercises cannot be stressed enough. Through these time-honored practices, we are able to work on timing for defenses, control of movements and targeting an actual human body with our punches and kicks.

Rick and I also combined our warm-up routine with working with the bo staff. It is amazing how much of a workout you can get, going back and forth practicing attacks and counter attacks with a bo. We are a far cry from the speed of Master Po and Cain in the opening sequence of the "Kung Fu" TV Series, (although I often have this in mind as we work back and forth...) but we are working slowly and deliberately. Speed will come.

I truly am thankful to be able to practice with Rick. For whatever reason, our school does not offer an adults only class, so being able to practice with someone my own age, who sees Martial Arts training the same way I do, has been a huge blessing to me.

So each day I work to get better, and I push forward to my Black Belt Goal.

Keeping in mind the words of Sang Kyu Shim, "If the martial arts practitioner concentrates on (or "invests in") one basic technique a day, striving for complete perfection, he will, after even one year, have accumulated a wealth of techniques that no money can buy and no thief can steal. The individual does not have these qualities so much as he is them."

STRENGTHEN WHAT REMAINS

Once when I was about seventeen years old, I was riding my bicycle home from a friend's house. It was late and dark outside with only streetlights to navigate by. But, I knew the city streets pretty well and had confidence I could easily get home.

I remember rounding a corner and hitting a patch of sand on the road. This caused my front wheel to hit a curb and abruptly turn sideways. I flew over the handlebars of my 10-speed bike, Superman style. Instinctively I tucked and rolled and landed rather impressed with myself.

I got up, walked over to my bike, twisted the handlebars back into place and rode home.

The next day I didn't even feel the bruises I had earned from my crash. My attitude was more like, "oh, yeah, I must have gotten that last night."

Oh to be young again.

Now it seems it doesn't take anything to make my body ache. Sit too long at the desk at work, sleep on a different pillow, twist wrong and a new pain introduces itself.

Injuries that I bounced back easily from in my forties simply linger in my fifties. Especially, I have learned, knee injuries.

That's the way it's been for me lately. My road to recovery with my knee and my hips has been a long one. It seems that stretching has almost become a necessity for moving well. I start each day on the stationary bike followed by stretching. Although I've graduated from barely making it around my building at work to walking during my lunch again, I never feel normal. Something always tightens or hurts.

When I started this black belt journey a little over two and a half years ago, the thought never occurred to me that I would not be able to do everything. Oh sure, I figured I may not be able to kick as high, or as fast, but I never saw myself as having any physical limitations. I never knew I could get injured so easily or take so long to recover.

Now I'm realizing some of the jumping and spinning kicks may be a part of my past. I have to be very careful and it's not easy. I'm still in a class full of teenagers. It's hard to back off when I need to.

It's not easy getting older. This part of my journey is not easy. Not by a long shot.

But I keep thinking of this one phrase, "Strengthen what remains." I have always held a life philosophy of not focusing on what I cannot do, but focusing on what I can. I'm not saying this is easy, but it is what I have to work with.

2018 is the year I turn fifty-three, and also the year I will earn my black belt. Currently I have two black tips on my deputy black belt. I need a total of five before I can test.

So now, what's my goal? What's my focus?

I will strengthen what remains. I will focus on what I can do.

I am working on the basics. I want a sharp-looking sidekick and round kick. These are kicks that show up in my poomsae. I've let them slack, as the twisting required has been almost impossible. But I'm ready to start working on them again. Slow tension kicks at first and then move into more power.

I also want the details of my technique to look sharper. I have noticed in class that when I come prepared already knowing the moves, the teachers give more attention to the details of techniques.

And most of all, when I finally get a chance to wrap that black belt around my waist, I want to feel like I have done my absolute best to earn it.

DAVID IANETTA

WHAT ONE MAN CAN DO, ANOTHER CAN DO!

Just a few months shy now of the three years mark of practicing Taekwondo, that Black Belt is solidly within reach.

Lately I've been reflecting on what I've been through so far.

Looking over the physical hurdles I've had to leap- just barely at times- over, I'm not sure if it stands as a testimony to my stubbornness or stupidity that I am still going strong.

Perhaps all men my age have to go through these challenges, we certainly cannot go around them.

There was the prostate cancer scare that dragged on for months, with doctor appointments, tests, and simply waiting. At the same time I had my heart looked at and they found an enlarged aorta that I'll have to have monitored once a year, forever. But I can't complain. I didn't have cancer and the heart issue could have been much worse. It was just the prolonged "not knowing" that played tricks with my mind for months, but through that, I went to class, I practiced, I advanced.

Then, of course, my famous knee issues that have never really gone away. Hips are doing better but my knees will never be the same. Old motorcycle injury for sure is a factor. Physical therapy was good, and educational.

Then who could forget my on again off again back issues? I missed a few classes these past weeks because of that. But I'm now combating this one with Pilates and weekly visits to my awesome Chiropractor.

Over these three years I've had times when I felt like I could go on forever and times when I really wanted to just give up. Nights when I felt encouraged after class and others when I just took a shower popped a few Advil and went to bed thinking "why am I doing this to myself?"

I stick with it through all this because I love it. I see the benefits and they outweigh the challenges. I picked up something I left behind many years ago and I have no plans of putting it down again.

So why am I sharing all this? The ups, the downs, and the physical challenges? Am I looking for a pat on the back? Should we be cuing some sad music while I look thoughtfully out the window as it rains? Maybe I want the "atta boy" and "you can do it!" accolades social media so easily provides these days?

I really am not looking for any of that.

I share all this now for the same reason I've been posting this blog for almost three years.

I want to show it is possible to keep going. If were one of those men who had zero physical problems and could do anything I wanted, that would be the anomaly.

I firmly believe I am not the exception, nor exceptional.

Like my favorite line from "The Edge" where Anthony Hopkins shouts, "What one man can do, another can do!"

For those of you who are thinking about starting at a, shall we say more advanced age, then believe me when I say:

You can do it. It is possible. If you've taken the first steps and begun Martial Arts training, keep going. If you are thinking about it, maybe now is the time to begin.

What one man (or woman) can do, another can do.

"THE REWARDS OF ACTION ARE TANGIBLE AND THE OPPORTUNITIES FOR ACTION ARE MANY."
- BRUCE LEE

It's funny how large an obstacle can become when we choose to avoid it. The longer we keep something at a distance, the more insurmountable the problem becomes.

For me that particular nemesis took the form of Taegeuk Chil Jan (number seven of the Taegeuk poomsae).

For some time now, I've been working on seven out of the eight Taegeuk poomsae forms on a regular basis.

I started doing this because at one point I realized I was forgetting each poomsae after testing for it. So over the past year I progressively added them to my weekend workouts, as they were needed for testing. Slowly the number grew.

When I earned my deputy black belt, I began having to test with them again, two at a time. First with one and two, next three and four and more recently I tested with Taeguk five and six for my third black tip.

One a side note, only two more of those black tips and I will become a black belt candidate. That black belt is getting closer!

But now I'm going to be testing on Taegeuk seven and eight. Eight I know because that was the first poomsae I kept practicing after I tested with it. But seven I have been avoiding. I haven't worked on Taegeuk Chil Jan for over a year or longer.

I've watched others perform it, even looked at it on YouTube. But when it came time to practice it, I kept putting it off.

I'm not sure what it was about this particular poomsae that kept me from working on it in my private practice, but there is something that just looked overly complicated and impossible for me to remember. Even though I tested on it once already, it was far gone from my memory.

I kept telling myself I would review it before I needed to know it in class, but I did not follow through. The knowledge that I would eventually have to face this poomsae nagged at me in the back of my mind.

Then I passed my third black tip test and I knew next class I would have to finally face my nemesis.

The time came for me to review the poomsae with Master Won. She asked me if I knew Chil Jan and I had to admit I could not remember it. I could see the surprise on her face, perhaps even disappointment.

In traditional Taekwondo, being taught a poomsae is actually treated as a gift from instructor to student. That principle is still ingrained in me. I felt like I neglected the gift.

Inwardly I kicked myself. Of course she smiled and began to re-teach it to me. Even encouraged me, saying it was a difficult one to learn. But I knew that I had let myself down.

I recently ran across a quote from Bruce Lee who said, "The rewards of action are tangible and the opportunities for action are many."

Basically we have numerous opportunities to get off our lazy butts and do something and when we do we always feel better for it.

I left the Do Jang feeling regret for my inaction, but I was determined to conquer my nemesis this weekend.

So Saturday came and I decided to work on nothing but Teaguk Chil Jan for my practice. I still wasn't looking forward to it. It had grown in my mind to an almost impossible task. I felt that it had some confusing steps in it that would take a lot of time to get right.

But I went into my personal Do Jang and began working on it, one step at a time..

It was slow going. I started from the beginning, over and over, gradually learning the next step. I'm not really sure how long I was out there, but eventually I got the flow down and that's when something amazing happened.

I started to love it.

First there is nothing in this poomsae that my bad knee will hinder. The front kicks and crescent kicks do not require the same twists as other kicks do and I am able to perform them equally with both legs. Also there are a lot of cool hand techniques involved that make it very interesting. The tiger stance is a great one for strengthening my knees so I'm getting a needed work out there.

I finished up feeling great, the hurdle was behind me.

But would I remember it next time I tried it?

When evening came, I decided to go at it again and see what I could remember from the morning's practice. I went out into the backyard and performed the poomsae over and over. I remembered every move.

This is a poomsae I really feel I can get into, to reach that level beyond just trying to remember the next moves. To climb inside it, forgetting everything else and just move effortlessly through it as a true expression of Wu Wei (effortless action)

And to think that by putting off the challenge, I've been putting of this awesome expression of movement.

That's the amazing thing about pursuing something like Taekwondo. It teaches us so many things about ourselves. No matter what the obstacle is, if we become determined to tackle it, breaking it down a step at a time if we have to, we can accomplish anything.

And sometimes the thing we dreaded becomes something we love.

Bruce Lee's quote is worth repeating, "The rewards of action are tangible and the opportunities for action are many."

MR. DAVID, I THINK HE IS TRYING TO KILL YOU!

I'm covered in sweat and my muscles are at the point of exhaustion. Master Ko has me performing a push-up drill. Do one push-up, stand up, then do two, stand, three stand, you get the idea… and keep going like that until you reach ten.

This came after we've done some warm-ups, stretching and pretty intense leg work with what looks like a huge rubber band.

Master Won is looking on as I have my private lesson with Master Ko. I look over at her and she laughs, "Mister David, I think he is trying to kill you!"

I laugh back; I know she's only joking, at least I hope so!

About five weeks ago I started weekly private lessons with Master Ko.

Master Ko is a 5th degree Kukkiwon black belt. He graduated from the Korean National Sports University and is a winner of four International Gold Medals.

He has also had five surgeries on his knees and therefore understands knee issues on a personal level. He is the perfect instructor for me, knowing just how to get my knees stronger and my overall technique better.

He works me hard from the moment I get there to the minute I leave.

It is said, "When the student is ready, the teacher appears." This has proven to be true in my life.

I don't think I was ready to take on this level of training before now. For the past three years I've worked hard with my black belt goal firmly in sight. But now, in just five short weeks, I feel as if the real work has only just begun.

So far, in addition to the conditioning work, there has also been work on my basic technique. We've covered stances, blocks, punching and some kicks. Master Ko assures me he has many plans for my training.

This new phase has been both challenging and rewarding. I'm already reaping the benefits of sharper technique and a stronger body.

I have realized I'm capable of working much harder than I have been. The formation of an indomitable spirit, spoken of so many times in Taekwondo training, takes an effort and dedication I haven't embraced up until this point.

But I really feel it's time to do so.

Bruce Lee once said, "If you always put limits on everything you do, physical or anything else, it will spread into your work and into your life. There are no limits. There are only plateaus, and you must not stay there, you must go beyond them."

I always liked that quote, maybe even used it in another blog post, but I never really understood it until now.

When I train by myself or even in a class full of students, it's easy to coast. But when someone else trains you there is no room for that. Your instructor gets to know you better. They see your weaknesses and they push you to improve.

Looking back on the past three years of Taekwondo training, with all I have been through and achieved, I feel it has all been to prepare me for this next level.

But it's a battle. There is a definite battle going on between my spirit and my body.

In his book, "Moving Zen – Karate as a way to gentleness," C.W. Nicol said "The Martial Artist must regard his body as a splendid tool for the spirit to use. The body should not be allowed to dominate the spirit." Nicol, who studied Shotokan in Japan, touches on the key to successful training.

If I want to succeed in my goals I have to focus my spirit to conqueror my body. The tool needs to be sharpened and brought under submission.

Basically I cannot allow laziness to affect my training.

Currently I have my fourth black tip on my deputy black belt. In August I will test for my fifth and final tip, and at that time (if all goes well) I will be invited to test for my black belt in October.

Now, armed with this new insight and aided by these sessions with Master Ko, my black belt goal is firmly within sight.

And as that black belt comes within tangible reach, I realize it truly won't be the end of this journey, only the beginning.

BLACK BELT CANDIDATE

It has been a very long road building up to this point.

This past weekend I passed my final test as a Deputy Black Belt earning a fifth belt tip. At the end of testing, Master Ko handed me a large envelope with my name on it. I have been invited to test for my Black Belt, officially making me a Black Belt Candidate.

Inside the envelope is a schedule full of extra classes and pre-test sessions I'm required to take over the next few months. My test day will be November 3rd, 2018.

A brief glance over the testing requirements shows me I'll be testing on all my poomsae, kicking techniques, 5 board-breaking techniques, sparring, physical endurance/strength tests, as well as Korean terminology and a written essay.

The judges may also ask for other random things during the test.

As the large letters indicate in our Do Jang, "A Black Belt is not purchased, it is earned." I've been told by my friend (and 3rd Dan Black Belt), "This test is grueling, at the end you'll know you earned your Black Belt."

The next two and a half months are going to be busy ones to say the least, as I prepare for this test.

Although I have been working toward this test for the past three years or more, I find when I think about the test, I'm a bit intimidated. It's one thing to perform all these things, and yet another to have to perform them in front of the watchful eyes of the judges.

Two and a half months feel like a very short time.

It's funny how the mind works. Part of me sees the amount of tasks I'll have to perform and thinks, "Why on earth did you sign up for this? Why did you choose to put yourself into this situation? You must be crazy to invite stress like this into your life."

But then another voice says to me, "Keep your eye on the prize, you are almost there, don't give up."

I guess there are two ways of living life. One is to avoid anything truly difficult to minimize discomfort and chance of failure. I've lived long enough to see people who keep to this philosophy. They are not all that fun to be around, and are usually the first to voice objections when I bring up Taekwondo or riding motorcycles.

I don't judge, to each their own, live and let live and all that.

But for me, to embrace life is to embrace risk. That is how we live a life fully alive.

I love the movie "Point Break" (both the new one and the remake). I know I'm supposed to root for the good guy FBI agent, but in this movie I find myself identifying more with the criminals.

Or at the very least, agreeing with their way of life.

Their philosophy can be summed up in one quote by the character Bodhi, "If you want the ultimate, you've got to be willing to pay the ultimate price. It's not tragic to die doing what you love. "

So here I go, pushing myself a little bit more each day. I am not taking my eyes off that prize.

Or, I die trying..

BLACK BELT
IT'S ONLY THE BEGINNG

I have to laugh when I look a photo taken of me at my Black Belt Test.

I'm flying high, fist ready to power though ten boards. My eyes are laser focused on the ten boards below. Those ten boards are what's standing between me and finally getting my black belt. In that moment my heart is racing and I know I have this. There is no doubt in my mind.

But to quote one of my favorite movies, The 13th warrior, "And things were not always thus."

The night before my black belt test, I was a wreck.

Friday night we had a pre-black belt test class. Maybe it was the fact that I am not used to doing poomsaes in a group setting, surrounded by young kids... But I kept forgetting the moves. I could not make myself focus.

Perhaps I even over-trained

I have been practicing a lot; group classes on Tuesdays and

Thursdays, private lessons with Master Ko on Wednesdays, Saturday practice with Rick (3rd Dan black belt who is my age) and Sunday poomsae practice in my home dojang. In addition to that, my work moved to a new building with a gym. Five days a week I was using my lunch to work on my condition training.

Bicycle, weights, stretching, repeat.

Whatever the reason, Friday night I made mistake after mistake and by the time I left the dojang my confidence was shot.

The battle now was truly in my mind. I saw myself screwing up in front of my wife and the whole school. How could I trust myself to remember what I'd learned?

But I started to back off the ledge talking to my wife and a few text messages from Rick got me back into reality.

I finally laughed at myself, what am I picturing? Do I see myself being summoned by the resounding sound of a massive gong? A giant drum beating a slow rhythm while I am marched to the lit center of dark chamber? An ominous voice announcing, "Begin!" as I engage into a life and death struggle fighting off ninjas?

I really have to do something about my imagination. I calmed down and simply decided to do my best.

The day of the test arrived. I walked onto the mat and was met by Rick who gave me a final pep talk and told me once again to relax. I slowly stretched and moved through my poomsaes to get my body warmed up.

The test finally began and we were called to sit and meditate. I slowly breathed in and out as Master Kim spoke soft words of encouragement to myself and the other students who were testing.

To my relief, when my name was finally called I would be performing my poomsaes, demonstrating my blocks using Korean terminology and basic stances, alone on the mat.

Void of distractions, I performed the poomsaes, one after another without mistakes, building my confidence. I could hear people clapping for me after I passed each one, and the encouraging sound of Rick cheering me on.

Ironically, I made one mistake during the last one after I started feeling relieved, thinking I'm almost there! Master Kim had me repeat that part of the form and I moved on. By now I was so relaxed the mistake did not bother me at all.

Next came kicking techniques and footwork that I did with the rest of the group. It was good to get my blood moving for the sparring that came next.

For sparring I was matched up with Chris, a young 3rd Dan testing for his 4th. I was feeling great and very pleased that after two rounds I did not run out of breath.

Next came breaking. I had to break three boards with a punch, three with a turning back kick and then three with a jump front kick. I was stressed performing the back kick, as I worried about my knee twisting. I broke through the first two, and then ran to break the last with the jump front kick

This was the toughest kick of them all. Three boards were held chest high. The challenge came not from the height, but the way the boards were held. For the other two breaks the boards are held on both edges creating an unmovable target, but these boards were held on only one edge, like someone handing you a plate of food. The challenge is you have to kick them very fast to make up for the lack of support.

I took a breath, let out a yell and ran.

I jumped. I kicked. I hurt my foot.

The boards did not break.

I stepped back a few feet, ignored my throbbing foot and tried again. This time I broke right through.

Now it was time for endurance. I had to first jog fifty times around the dojang. My much younger classmates began to literally run circles around me as each in turn finished long before I did. But I kept my own pace, happy that my knee allowed me to run at all, and that all the cardio I have been doing paid off. Soon it was just me running, followed by student instructors and a crowd cheering on the old guy! I felt like I was in the latest installment of the Rocky franchise!

100 sit-ups, 150 backups and 55 push-ups later brought us to that final moment.

This was the last challenge, the power break. I took a breath, focused on my target and with one hammer fist broke through the ten boards and accomplished my goal.

I was a black belt!

As I reflect on this journey, I realize that getting my black belt will not be the end; it truly is only the beginning. I have achieved so many benefits from Taekwondo in the areas of physical health, mental focus and spiritual strengthening that I know I will continue this path for the rest of my life.

At the beginning of every class we state the ten student commitments. The tenth is, "always finish what I start." For me, this is a commitment to continue daily in my study of Taekwondo for the rest of my life.

My advice to anyone, young or old who is considering taking up Taekwondo can best be expressed in the words of Master Sang Kyu Shim in his book, "The Making of a Martial Artist."

"Venture into the unknown of your potential; you will surely come out the victor."

Made in the USA
Columbia, SC
18 February 2020